minerva
WORK SOLUTIONS PLLC

50 Ways to Work Wiser
Science Based Leadership and Professional Development

50 Ways to Work Wiser

Minerva Work Solutions PLLC

2018

Fifty Ways to Work Wiser
Copyright © 2018 by Minerva Work Solutions, PLLC.
    Kathryn E. Keeton, Ph.D.
    William S. O'Keefe, M.S.
    Lacey L. Schmidt, Ph.D.
    Kelley J. Slack, Ph.D.
    Annette Spychalski, Ph.D.

Affinity Publication Services

ISBN: 978-1-98-854919-4

First Edition

Editor: Angela Koenig
Cover Design: Irish Dragon Designs
Production Design: Affinity Publication Services

TABLE OF CONTENTS

mɩnerʋa
WORK SOLUTIONS PLLC

Work deserves to be meaningful and effective.
We make it so by applying psychological science

ABSTRACT

50 practical leadership, teamwork, and professional development tips, based on psychological evidence, presented in two minutes bites by five world class coaches to help you #workwiser now.

WHY?

This book exists to help you work more wisely. We, at Minerva Work Solutions, recognize the investment we all make in our jobs (most of us spend at least a third of our adult life at work), and we know we can do more to help ourselves and our communities by promoting humane and effective work practices. We also know that most "effective work practices" are promoted and spread without any scientific evidence as to their benefits, and as scientists this distressed us. We have written this book to make some of the practical wisdom discovered via Industrial-Organizational Psychology, backed by scientific evidence, more accessible to all for the good of working humankind.

HOW TO USE THIS BOOK

In the interest of putting something into your hands to use exactly when you need it, we've boiled down our experience and research into 50 practical tips. Each tip is presented on one to two pages. We've also categorized these tips as primarily relevant for leadership development, teamwork, or general professional development topics (e.g., career visioning). Please do NOT read these tips in the order we have presented them. We suggest that you use the table of contents to find which tip most appeals to you and most addresses your challenges right now. By reading no more than three tips at a time, you give yourself ample opportunity to try the behaviors advocated in each tip before challenging your busy mind to remember more than necessary to achieve your immediate goals. When you require another tip, they're all right here for you to access as needed.

SECTION ONE: LEADERSHIP DEVELOPMENT

TIP 1. LEADERSHIP IS ABOUT EFFECTIVE LEADING BEHAVIORS

The reality is that it just isn't enough to have good leadership characteristics. In fact, when you look at the last eighty years and thousands of pages of advice on what makes an ideal leader, you will see a host of conflicting characteristics. Why has so much research failed to articulate a consistent model of effective leadership? Because princely leaders can still exhibit poor leadership behaviors, while even a pauper of a leader can exhibit effective leadership behaviors in a critical and memorable situation.

While we are data rich (and probably because we are so data rich and must sift through and interpret so much information), our modern work world is full of situational complexity and ambiguity. Leaders who manage complex and ambiguous situations well are memorable and sought after. As a result, models of effective leadership that rely on specifying what behaviors enable leaders to manage complex and ambiguous situations well present a better answer today than lists of effective or admirable leadership characteristics.

The good news is that anyone, of any personality, can learn effective leadership behaviors. Sure, it is harder for some of us, who are more introverted for example, to learn some of these behaviors, but we still can learn to do them when we need to be an effective (and inspiring) leader. Here is a small taste of the behaviors that our research shows help leaders manage more effectively in complex situations across industries:

- ➢ Proactively sets up the parameters of every meeting and formal conversation (e.g., "This is what we're here to talk about, this is how long we have, and this is what we need by the end.")
- ➢ Repeatedly and explicitly invites input from others
- ➢ Repeats primary priorities and concerns until acknowledged by others
- ➢ Verbally offers recommendations and the rationale for those recommendations
- ➢ Asks questions whenever any team member appears unsure or concerned
- ➢ Directly invites others to question and add to rationale
- ➢ Delegates authority for responsibilities (not tasks) to high performers and high-potential team members

TIP 2. DELEGATE RESPONSIBILITIES

What is the biggest difference in the capabilities needed to be an executive instead of a middle manager? One of the most telling differences in capabilities is how someone delegates. Managers delegate tasks; Leaders delegate responsibilities.

Of course, it is not as simple as switching from telling folks to get certain tasks done to directing them to take ownership of whole projects or efforts. Delegating responsibilities well requires you to use these emotionally intelligent behaviors:

1) **Know to whom you are delegating, their capabilities, and what motivators they value right now.** An abundance of research evidence shows that authoritative influence is the least effective and most relationship-damaging way to tell someone what to do. Persuasive power is much more influential, effective, and relationship building. Persuasive influence depends on knowing what services others can and will exchange with you to value your priorities.

2) **Explicitly set up learning and performing expectations.** Expectations that are defined as SMART (specific, measurable, achievable, realistic, and time-bound) work best, but it is even more important to set up both a learning and performance expectation so that you can professionally develop others. Psychological research reveals that learners frequently learn what they are told to expect they will learn. Also, performers more frequently exceed expectations when they know exactly what behaviors constitute meeting your expectations, and what behaviors would help them exceed your expectations. One other hint: if you need to articulate what constitutes ineffective performance, then you are delegating responsibility to the wrong person–that person isn't capable right now.

3) **Articulate what resources are available and what constitutes fair play.** Delegates cannot start owning a responsibility until they are aware of where to get the necessary information, materials, labor, facilities, and allies. If you do not have the time to show delegates where the resources are, then you must plan for and allow them the time necessary for them to discover these things before they take ownership. One of the most common methods for doing this is to have a delegate shadow you or another subject-matter expert for a designated period. It is also important to articulate what legal, professional, and ethical codes apply to this responsibility. It is impossible for delegates to intentionally play fair if

they are unaware of the rules, and most legal and ethical infractions will reflect directly on the delegating leader's executive credibility (i.e., yours).

4) **Declare a state of emergency procedure.** What should the delegates do if they encounter a problem they don't know how to address? How long do you want them to struggle with it on their own before bringing it to your attention? When do you require them to ask for help? How? From whom first? Research shows that defining a basic emergency procedure minimizes errors, saves time and money, and increases delegates' self-efficacy and satisfaction with your leadership.

5) **Require delegates to publicly own the responsibility and the credit.** Take a tip from social psychology: nothing guarantees personal commitment to an idea or endeavor as much as announcing to others that you're supporting that idea or endeavor. Have delegates make that meeting announcement or send out that email with your introduction and support. Likewise, when delegates achieve success it is important not just to publicly praise them, but also to have them publicly accept praise and congratulations for their work. Otherwise, no one will take ownership for the next responsibility you delegate.

Tip 3. Don't leave them wondering what you want while you act

Learning to lead, even situationally (like when you are the content expert in the room), is challenging for many professionals. Most of us learn what leadership looks like vicariously. We see a whole lot of ineffective command or directive-style leadership behaviors as the norm, and not the efficient leadership behaviors that psychology indicates are more effective. Fortunately, a little coaching can help you discover and learn to leverage better leadership behaviors quickly. Among the many such behaviors is learning to state your intentions before acting. In fact, this is literally what it means to give others a lead, to tell them where you are trying to go, what you are trying to accomplish. From our experience advising professionals working in extreme and high-stakes environments, we found that one of the quickest and simplest ways to build a shared understanding and coordinate group efforts is to require every team-member to state his/her intention to do something before doing it. For example, a surgeon who tells the surgical team that he intends to close the patient next allows those assisting the operation to put the right instruments to the forefront of the surgeon's operating surface; and, it signals everyone around the patient to search for and remove any hazards to closing the patient before those hazards become deadly (e.g., leaving a sponge inside the incision line).

Stating your intentions before taking action allows the rest of your team to:

> ➢ Get into position to back up your decision.
> ➢ Check your thinking for errors before you commit to a disastrous course.
> ➢ Carry out your assignment/complete your tasks even if you are distracted, interrupted, or removed from the project.

Here is an example from my own experience. I announced to the rest of our management team that I was going to pull our financial data at noon today so that I could use it to build my monthly report to the board on Monday. Announcing I intended to pull the data today reminded one of our project managers that payment for a major consulting project will not be received until tomorrow and we realized the resulting profit would not show up in my report. I could then make a more informed choice about whether I wanted to pull the data at noon as planned and explain the apparent discrepancy in projected and actual profits; or, I could wait to pull the data and compile my report just before the meeting. Had I not communicated my intentions, I might have presented an apparent profit loss to the board without any explanation or understanding as to why the discrepancy existed. Communicating my intentions encouraged my project manager to contribute useful information in return and that information made me look like a much wiser leader.

TIP 4. BLEND LEADERSHIP STYLES

By default, everyone has a preferred leadership style and a preferred circle of influence based on the type of power that best fits your personality. For example, if you are very extroverted, you may prefer using a charismatic style and transformational techniques to influence management circles. But a purely charismatic style is not the most effective way to lead a major auditing project for a traditionally staid and hierarchically-oriented blue-chip accounting firm. Techniques and styles are more effective as they are blended to leverage more of the values of the people and organizations involved in a given situation. Sometimes this means adding a little to your preferred leadership patterns of behavior; and other times, it means blending multiple styles and techniques from completely outside of your comfort zone. As you are learning and when you are under stress, you will rely on your preferred leadership style more—and this will limit your leadership effectiveness until you become aware of when it's happening. Then you can choose the right blend from an array of learned styles and techniques.

So how do you learn? We recommend using all five of these approaches:

1) Start asking your mentors questions about how and why they blend leadership styles and techniques.
2) Get feedback from others about how your leadership style is perceived.
3) Learn how to ask good questions to help you discover what others value and hope to accomplish at work.
4) Get experiential training.
5) Get coaching so you can learn about and practice blending different leadership styles and techniques.

Knowing the answer to effective leadership is simple. Doing it is harder. It requires blending your leadership styles and techniques to best accommodate the values of the people and organizations you work with to accomplish a greater good for all.

Tip 5. Respect the Power of Introverted Leaders

In Western societies, a common stereotype of an effective leader is a gregarious, charismatic, action-oriented individual who easily engages with people of multiple types. Many extroverted leaders naturally demonstrate these characteristics, and it's easy for more introverted people to question whether they are suited for leadership roles. Introverts certainly can behave in more extroverted ways, but this often requires additional effort on their part. Moreover, asking introverts to act like extroverts means missing the opportunity to leverage their natural strengths.

Susan Cain has explored this area in recent years. She describes how introverts can excel in leadership roles when they leverage their tendencies to listen more than speak, preference for working alone, and comfort with letting others run with their ideas. For example, effective creative and strategic thinking often requires the solitude and contemplation that introverts prefer. Extroverts are generally more inclined to move quickly and brainstorm with others. Introverts are also more likely to carefully consider their ideas and associated risks before launching into a plan of action that may have unintended negative consequences (actions that an extroverted leader may be inclined to pursue). In addition, when working with others, introverts can leverage their listening skills to foster collaboration among team members and to maximally engage them in joint tasks. More extroverted leaders may have to curb their desire to enthusiastically participate in and drive the discussion.

Successful leadership takes many forms. The key to leveraging the strengths that diverse leaders can offer is to become the best leadership version of yourself versus attempting to model your approach after someone you are not.

TIP **6.** LEAD BY EXAMPLE WHEN IT COMES TO RULES

We are all familiar with the saying, "leaders LEAD by example," but research evidence supports that leading by example can also reduce the number of errors made by employees. Let's look at Leroy and colleagues' (2012) study for more insight into which leader behaviors make the saying true.

Among a large sample of nurse teams (54 to be exact), fewer errors were made when their leaders did two important things: 1) leaders followed the rules themselves, and 2) leaders ensured others followed the rules.

Note that leading by example specifically refers to following rules, requesting others to follow the rules you follow, and recognizing your colleagues and subordinates for following and encouraging others to follow rules. Doing so engages positive peer pressure (instead of less effective authoritative sources of power) and influences more broadly by using your social network to spread a healthy behavior trend. In such cases, leading by example really can be an effective tool to guide your employees' behavior and improve your bottom line in a real and measured way (like improving patient care and reducing mortality rates in hospitals).

15

The study referenced is:

Leroy, H., Dierynck, B., Anseel, F., Simons, T., Halbesleben, J. R. B., McCaughey, D., Savage, G. T., & Sels, L. (2012). Behavioral integrity for safety, priority of safety, psychological safety, and patient safety: A team-level study. *Journal of Applied Psychology*, 97, 1273-1281.

TIP 7. USE A COORDINATION STRUCTURE TO LEAD ALL MEETINGS

Tired of leading boring, pointless meetings and telling people the same things over and over? Frustrated because your employees refuse to take ownership or act on priorities no matter how many times you meet to present them? Many such problems and challenges arise because there isn't a coordination structure in place. Fortunately, anyone can implement a coordination structure, and one of the simplest such structures we've seen among ultra-high performing teams is easy to learn: The 2 x 2 x 2.

In a 2 x 2 x 2 meeting, every leader has 5 minutes to briefly state her two biggest concerns today, her two major projects or accomplishments impacting this week, and the two resources/help she needs most this week. To do this, each leader must come prepared to talk about their 2 x 2 x 2s, and should write them down at least 15 minutes before the meeting. Structuring meetings this way makes the most of our limited attention spans by focusing our time and energy where it counts the most. It also allows team members to form a shared picture of what leaders are working on and why, and it enables better management of shared resources and enables more helping behaviors to occur.

For example: "My two biggest concerns today are dealing with our product shortage, and meeting the repair deadline on our faculty cafe's freezer today. We did manage to get all our kitchen employees 'Safe2Serve' certified last week, which is a major accomplishment. That helps toward making us ready for the national hospital health inspection next month which is the only major project I'm focused on right now. For helps, I still need supervisors to make sure that we are recording temperatures in the logs for every refrigerator and freezer on site at least eight times daily on even hours. I also still need approval from accounting to purchase the rest of the personnel protection equipment required to meet hospital standards for the lobby cafe."

You may not always have exactly 2 concerns or 2 major projects or need 2 helps (sometimes it might be 1 x 3 x 2, or 5 x 1 x 0, or etc.), but try to keep it to 6 points total and cover all three areas:

1) Big concerns today.
2) Major projects or accomplishments that might impact other leaders' efforts.
3) Help you need to address big concerns or further your major projects.

It works best if every leader endeavors to use the 2 x 2 x 2, but even if I am the only leader doing so, at least my priorities and needs are clearer for coordination and I've enabled others to support my initiatives. A final tip: others are more likely to help if you name who you want to help and tell them how you want them to help you, why, and what you are trying to accomplish (e.g., aww Tip 8 about RRI: Recommendation, Rationale, Intention).

TIP 8. IF YOU WANT PEOPLE TO FOLLOW, THEY NEED TO KNOW YOUR RRI

If you want to work well with others, then you need a communication protocol. The term "protocol" sounds daunting but it simply means an official procedure for doing something. A communication protocol is a procedure for sharing information (usually verbally) between two entities. The good news is that effective protocols are not complicated, and one of the most effective communication protocols for ensuring you communicate sufficient content to achieve your initiative in every conversation at work boils down to just 3 letters: RRI (Recommendation, Rationale, Impact).

➢ **Recommendations** refers to saying what you want done.
➢ **Rationale** is explaining your logic behind your recommendation, or saying why you want something done.
➢ **Impact** is projecting into the future and saying what you are ultimately trying to accomplish or avoid by doing something now.

Our Recommendation: Use the communication protocol known as RRI (Recommendation, Rationale, Impact) in all conversations (e.g., meetings, e-mails, phone calls, chats, etc.) to increase the efficiency of your information exchanges, reduce frustration with others for not telling you enough, strengthen memories, and decrease the likelihood of errors due to misunderstandings and missing information (Rationale). Communication protocols are part of a group of best practices that increase employee productivity by around $5,200 per employee per year when used by every member of an organization (Impact).

For Example: I tell Alex I want her to build two versions of her marketing report, one monthly dashboard-style report for the board, and one weekly report for the management team (Recommendation). I think that the weekly detail is more information than the board really wants to know, and the board doesn't have time to review so much detail in the meeting–which they will do if we give it to them (Rationale). Limiting the board's view to the dashboard for the month will still let them debate our marketing progress while giving them 10-15 more minutes to talk marketing strategies with us (Impact). (If my rationale is faulty, this gives Alex a chance to tell me why before we try it. If my predicted impact is wrong, then Alex and I both will remember why we are doing it, and either one of us can spot when my recommendation isn't working as expected and should probably be changed or at least re-debated).

Another Example from an Extreme Environment /Critical Operations: The Fire Scene Commander directs

Engine 52 to enter the building from the backdoor to search the break-room for unconscious employees (Recommendation) because a manager reports two employees who were on break when the fire broke out are still missing (Rationale) and the back entrance opens directly into the break-room allowing for the quickest access to the search area (Impact). If the back entrance is engulfed in flames, this allows for the Captain of Engine 52 to quickly inform the Commander that search access is too dangerous from that route and to suggest another solution to accomplish the initiative of saving two lives."

Packaging your communications (i.e. speaking, e-mailing, calls) in a consistent format or according to a protocol, like RRI, helps you prioritize and set initiatives more quickly, and minimizes miscommunication by helping others learn what information to expect from you, as well as identify when you haven't given them that information or when they didn't understand it, and then ask you for clarifications directly. When communicating in a hurry or under time-pressure, starting with your recommendation and your rationale for it also facilitates faster, better-quality decision-making.

TIP 9. BE A GOOD DECISION-MAKING LEADER BY LEARNING DIFFERENT DECISION MODELS

As a team leader, you are the final decision maker. How do you make sure that you are making good decisions? If you are going to be confident in selecting your team's ultimate course of action, there are at least three methods of decision making that you should be familiar with and should consider how to use well.

One method is **Codified Decision Making (CDM)**, where the decisions are pre-planned, and documented or codified. CDM can be a document saying if A happens, do B. NASA's Mission Control at the Johnson Space Center has volumes of CDM, labeled "Flight Rules." If a situation covered in Flight Rules occurs, the flight director knows what decision s/he should make. (FYI: the flight director can and must deviate from Flight Rules if s/he believes the circumstances dictate another decision.) The benefit of CDM is the decisions were made when time for detailed analysis and discussions was available. They are also good in time-critical situations when the decision maker does not have time to do a lot of thinking. An example in the airline world is engine failure during take-off. The pilot does not have time to analyze the situation and make benefit/cost/risk trades. Instead, s/he relies on a codified rule: if the engine fails below a certain speed, abort; if the engine fails above that speed, continue the take-off. Also, CDM is easier to train and easier for less experienced decision makers to use. The problem with CDM is that it is impossible to cover every possible situation. If the organization doesn't want decision makers applying CDM improperly, the codified decisions must explain to what situations they apply (and by exclusion, to which they don't), and the rationale. To improve CDM, you improve the codified decisions, which has value up to the point that the documentation becomes too unwieldy to use.

A second decision-making method is **Analytical Decision Making (ADM).** ADM is the method taught in most decision-making courses where the decision-maker weighs various options, possibly even coming up with a weighting system. For example, since Option A has the lowest cost you give it 9 points, and since Option C has the highest cost, it gets 1 point. You then weigh all the criteria, e.g., benefits, ease, speed, risk, etc., and count all the values for each option. If Option B has the most points, that is the one you pick. ADM has value if you have the time and data, and if you must prove to a superior that you looked at all options and picked the best one. ADM is a process used to determine the right decision for codified decisions. A problem with ADM is that you must have the time and the data. Also, some of the weights seem arbitrary. For example, unless you have very detailed engineering data, how do you evaluate risk? Instead of points, you could use a relative ranking of HIGH, MODERATE or LOW, but that is subjective. Also, after adding up the points, some decision makers won't like the "winning" option (it doesn't feel right) and change the weights until they get the option they want. To improve ADM, you need to give decision makers time, good data, and organizationally accepted criteria and weights.

Another decision-making method is **Naturalistic Decision Making (NDM).** Based on experience and training, the decision maker already knows what decision to make: the "been there, done that, got the badge" decision-making process. NDM is one of the reasons that decision makers trying to use the ADM process may change the weights to get a different answer if experience tells them what the right decision is. Decision makers using NDM might run a short "mental simulation" of how the decided course of action will play out. If it works out fine, they will go with it. If the mental simulation shows a problem, they will either amend the course of action or possibly pick another. NDM is fast, works in complex situations, and in the hands of experts is correct. The problem with NDM is it takes true experts, people with lots of experience in different situations. Take the example of two drivers: Joe, who has driven the same route to work a thousand times, and Jane, who has driven a hundred different routes once. Which one is better qualified to evaluate a route neither has seen before? Too often inexperienced decision makers think they have seen a situation before, and therefore know the right decision to make. The problem is the situation is slightly different and the inexperienced decision maker doesn't see it. To improve NDM, you need to give decision makers more experiences.

In any given situation, you may need to use any one, or some blend of all three, of these decision-making methods, so it is important to know about each of them and do some proactive thinking about how their limitations and advantages match your usual and emergency work contexts. Research shows that your decision-making quality improves significantly as you learn to think and talk abstractly about the decision-making process with your team members and colleagues.

TIP 10. USE EVIDENCE-BASED MANAGEMENT TO MAKE ORGANIZATIONAL-LEVEL DECISIONS WELL

In Evidence-Based Management: The Basic Principles, organizational experts Eric Barends, Denise Rousseau, and Rob Briner have identified six critical steps to take before you make a decision.

1) Ask a Question that Can Be Answered.
   In order to use the scientific method, you must have a question. Identifying an issue is a good start, but then you need to translate that issue into an answerable question. So, instead of simply declaring that customer satisfaction is too low, ask yourself, "Which two changes can I make that will have the biggest impact on customer satisfaction?"
2) Collect Evidence.
   For organizations, evidence can come from four sources: Scientific literature (empirical studies), Professionals (people educated in organizational science like us), Internal organizational data, and Stakeholders (those who will be affected by the proposed change). Be both thorough and systematic in your search for evidence.

3) Determine the Quality of the Evidence.
Not all the evidence you collect will be of equal quality. Determine which pieces of evidence are of high quality and forget the rest.

4) Consider All of the Quality Evidence.
Sometimes we tend to focus on the most salient piece of evidence. The manager who stops by your office every day to complain about lost sales and blames the losses on sales reps being rude on the phone is likely to be remembered when you are looking at the evidence. Resist your impulse to give any one source of evidence too much weight. Pull together all the quality evidence and come up with one aggregated body of evidence.

5) Use the Quality Evidence when Making Decisions.
Sometimes we see clients who ignore all the evidence and make a decision based on no more than gut. We acknowledge that statistically if you roll the dice enough, eventually a winning roll will turn up. However, the "gut" can lie; good quality evidence doesn't. Make your decisions based on the quality evidence you spent effort and time collecting and aggregating.

6) Evaluate the Outcome of the Decision.
After you have applied the decision you've made based on that quality evidence, don't forget to go back and assess whether it needs to be tweaked. Use these same six steps to help you determine the efficacy of decisions you implemented.

TIP 11. FOLLOWERSHIP MUST BE MODELED REPEATEDLY

Being a good team member is more than blind obedience to the leader's direction. A good team member must inquire when s/he doesn't understand what the leader said or wants. In addition, s/he must advocate and even be assertive if s/he believes the leader has made a decision that has adverse safety or goal impacts. This is sometimes known as managing your manager, or leading your leader.

A valuable follower should ask questions about:
Situation: "What is happening?"
Goal: "Why are we doing this?"
Plan: "How will we do this?"
Role: "What do you want me to do?"

Team members must feel comfortable about asking questions when they don't have the same mental model (i.e. understanding of the situation) as the leaders, or disaster may ensue. It is important for leaders to say something like: "If you don't understand something, ask. I'd rather spend a few seconds answering a question than have you do something wrong. Besides there is a chance that the reason you don't understand is because you know or see something that I don't."

Once team members have a shared understanding of the situation, they still may have a different opinion on what should be done. Based on experience and training, a team member might have a different mental model of what needs to be done. Since you don't want blind obedience or "yes men or women," you want your team members to feel comfortable providing a recommendation or advocating an alternative course of action. If the team member feels strongly that the plan might have adverse safety or goal impacts, you want your team members to be assertive—to continue to advocate until s/he is sure the team understands the risk and makes a well-thought-out decision before continuing. To encourage and create a safe team climate where good followership can happen, you might say something like, "You are the expert in your area. When there is a problem, I expect you to provide and if necessary defend a recommendation."

There are many reasons why a team member may not be assertive. The problem could be an environment with a high authority gradient (the difference in authority between the leader and the team member). Depending on the authority gradient, team members "mitigate" or tone down their advocacy/ assertion.

There are 6 levels of mitigation:

1) Command: "Run the procedure now!"

2) Joint obligation statement: "I think we need to run the procedure."
3) Joint suggestion: "Why don't we run the procedure?"
4) Query: "Would you like me to run the procedure?"
5) Preference: "I think it would be smart to run the procedure."
6) Hint and Hope: "Isn't the equipment getting a little warm?"

Not all levels of mitigation are equally effective (as you probably surmise). Safe, highly-reliable operations usually require everyone to use the first three levels of mitigation consistently. The NASA Shuttle program had guidance on how to assert well:

1) Get the person's attention.
2) State your concern by leading with, "I have an immediate/grave/safety concern."
3) State the problem.
4) State the solution you have in mind.
5) Assertively, but respectfully, ask for a response which may be, "What do you think?"

The NASA Shuttle model is very similar to the DESC model in healthcare:

D—Describe the specific situation or behavior; provide concrete data.

E—Express how the situation makes you feel/what your concerns are.

S—Suggest other alternatives and seek agreement.

C—Consequences should be stated in terms of impact on established team goals.

Improper mitigation may result in the assertion getting lost to a busy/distracted leader. Many accidents have happened because the team member has hinted and hoped, and the leader didn't pick up on the concern. In the healthcare profession, they have come up with CUS, a set of buzzwords so that when a leader hears the buzzword, s/he knows that the team member is advocating/asserting a safety/goal success issue. CUS stands for:

"I am Concerned! I am Uncomfortable! This is a Safety Issue!"

Yet another technique for healthcare is the "2 Challenge Rule": a follower has an obligation to inquire/advocate/assert twice to ensure the leader addresses the concern (NOTE: failure of the leader to address the concern is assumed to mean that the leader did not hear/understand it).

Any of these techniques will help you lead your leader well, and once you have inquired, advocated, and even asserted, the leader will more likely make a good decision.

TIP 12. THE POORLY UNDERSTOOD ART OF EMPLOYEE DISCIPLINE

Forget the common definition of punishment, and even the less common (but more scientific) definition of punishment made famous by behavioral psychology. Discipline and punishment are necessary but insufficient tools, and are rarely used well. We tend to use authoritative punishment as a last resort of absolute desperation, usually when we're scared by an employee's behavior and the likely consequences of that behavior. Even then the punishment rarely works like we want. Leaders who are parents already know this reality from experience. So when you seriously need to correct an employee's behavior what actually works?

Discipline with positive framing.

Discipline with positive framing means that you may still need to use punishment, but you will also engage in helping the employee re-shape behaviors to achieve more success—as opposed to using punishment only to avoid disaster. The heart of discipline with positive framing consists in giving purposeful and encouraging corrective feedback. I'll give you an overly simplistic but illustrative example:

Jane crossed the street without looking both ways and her mother responded, "Jane, look both ways every time you cross the street so that we're sure to cross safely even when we're in a hurry. I know you can help us stay safe."

Does it sound like discipline with positive framing comes from a third-grade class room? Yes, it does, but if it works so well with 30 plus unruly third graders, then why can't it work for your business, too?

Let's walk through a more work-related example of how to give your discipline more positive framing:

Joe drives a dump-truck route through a congested neighborhood every week, and frequently forgets to watch for pedestrians when making right turns at red lights. This morning Joe hit a pedestrian while making a turn and broke the pedestrian's arm. Policy already dictates Joe will be suspended without pay for 7 days, and that Joe must take defensive driving and "intern" in the passenger seat of his truck for another 6 months. Then he can return to driving in a probationary capacity. The punishment is in place and even some of the behavioral modification, but not the positive framing. From Joe's perspective, all of this is so that he won't make a mistake again, and hopefully, no one will be hurt again by him. Of course, Joe is already motivated to avoid disaster and punishment, but positive framing gives Joe even more motivation (keep reading to find out how).

There are four steps to discipline with positive framing:

1) **Stay in the present and emphasize how the employee can do better.** Example: "Joe, sit in this truck and talk through a perfectly safe drive with me. Show me the best pedestrian check in the world."

2) **Insist your employee wants to be competent (even when the employee disagrees or is obstinate).** Example: "We don't have time right now to get into why it happened or what is wrong with the company (your life, our relationship, etc.). We have just enough time to figure out how to do this better and keep getting better at it."

3) **Share the responsibility for discipline and improvement with your employee.** Example: "Joe, I need you to turn this mistake and the accident into something we can all learn from—tell me how you're going to turn this into something that can help us all do better and better."

4) **In addition to setting those SMART goals, give simple encouragement.** Example: "I want to hear about two things you are going to do to help us safeguard our drives in congested neighborhoods when you return from the suspension. I believe you can become our expert on driving these tough routes, so let me know if you come up with anything else that might help."

Finally, please don't forget that a large part of being an effective leader is learning how to be an influential coach. This means you will have to take our four suggested steps for discipline with positive framing and figure out how they can be tailored to your operating context so that they maximize your positive influence.

Tip 13. Focus on the Gist of Leading Teams

If a leader wants a team to work together effectively, she has some very specific responsibilities:

1) Setting Expectations,
2) The Team Climate,
3) "Synching" the Team
4) Deferring to Expertise.

The **first** responsibility of a leader is to set expectations. One key expectation is that all team members must use their team skills if they are to work interdependently to accomplish the goal. The leader could say: "I expect each team member to communicate what he or she sees and what it might mean, to resolve constructively any conflict in those assessments, to develop and defend a team recommendation, and to work together to accomplish our plan while looking out for each other." Once the leader sets these expectations, s/he must be a role model, i.e., walk the team skills walk, and mentor team members who don't meet the expectations.

The **second** responsibility of a leader is to establish the team climate. For example, it is safe to voice a risky/

conflicting opinion, or it is safe to admit mistakes without being worried about punishment.

A very short team briefing, "I will make mistakes, you all help me; you will make mistakes, the rest of the team and I will help you," would establish the climate that admitting mistakes is okay and that the team is there to support each other. Also by stating that the leader is not perfect, s/he is making it easier for team members to inquire, advocate, and assert. By "inquire," I mean a team member feels safe to ask questions when s/he doesn't understand the situation or the leader's intent. By "advocate and assert," I mean a team member feels safe to make and defend a recommendation. The mark of a good team climate is not one which rewards someone who "halts the presses" when s/he was right, but rather thanks the person who halts the process even when s/he was wrong! If that person is instead "counseled" to have all the data before acting, that person and probably others will never speak up unless they are 110% sure they are right. Unfortunately, by then it might be too late.

The **third** responsibility of a leader is to "synch" the team. The one constant is change. No matter how well you plan and prepare, something in environment or system or whatever will not be as expected. So, the goal or plan might have to change. Another way to define "synching" is, as things change, for the leader who is responsible to make sure every team member understands the new situation or goal or plan and their part in it. An example of synching might be: "Team, we are behind schedule due to the failure. We are re-prioritizing our tasks. We need to do Task C first.

That means Joe has to hold off what he is doing, and Jane has the lead. When Task C is done, we will re-evaluate where we are and what to do next. Any questions? Anyone see any problems with that plan?"

The **fourth** responsibility of a leader is to "defer to expertise." No one on a team has all the knowledge and skills to accomplish the task. If someone did, there would be no reason to have a team. Each member has his or her own unique knowledge, skills, and experiences. A leader must realize that depending on the circumstances, any team member might be the "smartest person in the room," the one who best knows what is happening and what should be done. That person may be the newest member on the team. Here is an example from my world of International Space Station operations: if there ever is a fire on-board, the "smartest person in the room" is the flight controller responsible for the life support system. The leader, the Flight Director, must realize that the flight controller has the best situation awareness and should have the best plan. That does not mean the leader abdicates decision making to the team member; the final decision always rests with the leader. It does mean that the leader will not overweigh the recommendation of the most senior person or the one with the most impressive title, but listen to the person who has the most intimate knowledge of what is happening, regardless of rank.

SECTION TWO: TEAMWORK SKILLS

TIP 14. FACILITATED DEBRIEFS CREATE CONTINUAL IMPROVEMENT IN TEAMS

The dust is settling. Your team finished the project, at least for now. You gather in your conference room for a debriefing of what went wrong. After all, that is the best way to improve performance next time. Or is it? Enter the Facilitated Debrief.

Team Leadership and Debriefing Failures

If you only focus on what went wrong, even in a "let's fix this next time" way, your team won't improve as much as it could. Focusing on faults, failures, and deficiencies alone is like trying to coach basketball by explaining what plays not to run. It is a failure of leadership that results in poor team performance and that disables continual improvement.

That doesn't mean leaders should not debrief their teams after an event, or talk about what should be better. But you need to handle that debrief in the right way to be productive.

One of the biggest responsibilities of a leader, and keys to leading well, is facilitating continuous improvement. Research indicates that well-conducted facilitated debriefs are one of the best ways to do so. Simply put, if you want to win more as a team, then use a structured facilitated debrief after every major project. Facilitated debriefs are appropriate after many events, from the completion of a large project to board meetings just to name two.

What is a Facilitated Debrief?

Facilitated debriefs are different from typical debriefs. "Facilitated" means that the leader focuses on asking the whole team "what, why, and how" questions. And the whole team analyzes the project outcome.

When leading a facilitated debrief, the leader does not offer his or her evaluation of the situation or recommendations until after the team has offered theirs. In fact, you know you are doing it right when your team members do most of the talking, and even the typically quiet team members start to offer effective recommendations without a direct invitation.

Let me reiterate that: In a facilitated debrief, the team evaluates the team. The team leader simply facilitates that evaluation.

The Benefits of a Facilitated Debrief

➢ Teams who master facilitated debriefs:
➢ Have shared definitions of what effective teamwork is.
➢ Leverage individual performance strengths effectively.
➢ Admit and correct for errors before they contribute to disasters.
➢ Demonstrate focused improvement on previously set goals.
➢ Report increased confidence in their team.
➢ Generalize lessons learned to new performance situations.

Leading a Facilitated Debrief

The goal of a facilitated debrief is to have team members discuss what went right and wrong. The team should also discuss how individual actions affected other team members, and the final project outcome. Facilitated debriefs work best when the leader encourages team members to interact well.

Team members should address each other directly and the team. Your ability to continue to learn and self-correct your team depends on establishing a safe learning climate. To do this, you will need to remember that titles and status are irrelevant during debriefs, and that you must participate and encourage others to do so.

The debrief should analyze why situations happened (good or bad), seeking the root cause. Think about what events contributed to the outcome and what behaviors influenced those events. Offer behavioral examples for discussion by the team.

What to Discuss

1) **Discuss how different individual team members were affected by others' actions.** What did they do that helped you? What information or help do you wish you were given by others?
2) **Discuss what each team member was thinking.** Explain your rationale for doing or not doing something. What was your understanding of what was happening at the time, and how was that accurate and inaccurate?
3) **Discuss what went well and why.** What did the team do right that it should keep doing?
4) **Discuss what could be improved and how.** What could be done differently to make teamwork easier in similar situations next time?
5) **what factors enabled or impeded success.** What obstacles to teamwork were inherent in the situation? How could the team work around these in the future? What situational factors contributed to the team's success and how could the team leverage

these in similar future situations? Are there tools to improve the team performance?

6) **Discuss how to apply the team's learning to future projects.** Concentrate on finding two to three new things you can do, or tools you can use, to ensure you work well on teams tomorrow in any situation.

Learning to Lead a Facilitated Debrief

A short example with a team of four floor nurses:

<u>Facilitator/Charge Nurse</u> asks, "Was there a time when anyone felt like they didn't have the right information at the right moment?"

<u>Nurse 1</u> answers, "At the start of the shift, I wasn't entirely clear on what the monitoring orders were for two of my patients, and combing through their charts took my head out of game for several minutes while a transfer was arriving."

<u>Nurse 2</u> adds, "Some complications with the transfer definitely distracted me for a while, too, but Jay (Nurse 3) proactively volunteered to keep eyes on two of my patients closest to his, and that helped give me the head-space I needed to settle our transfer."

<u>Nurse 1</u> says, "That was a good thing because I was definitely too distracted to know what was going on and be of any help."

<u>Facilitator</u> asks, "This will happen again tomorrow. What helped today that we can do again to make things go smoothly despite the chaos tomorrow?"

<u>Nurse 3</u> answers, "Maybe we could ask the outgoing shift to bullet main orders for us on the lounge white board, so we at least have a starting point for understanding them, and we can help each other chase down doctors for clarifications as needed."

<u>Nurse 2</u> replies, "And we can play zone defense, like Jay and I did today, when it's practical, so that one of us has more head-space to focus on settling in a complicated transfer."

<u>Facilitated</u> debriefs take a little practice to master. Especially on a critical project, emotions can run high. With strong leadership, a little teamwork training to support them, and a consistent structure they are a powerful leadership tool. They will help you build a more engaged and talented team.

TIP 15. DEFINE TEAMWORK FOR YOUR TEAM

Are your people a team or just a group? Is there a difference? Is the difference important?

The answer to the last two questions is yes.

According to teamwork expert, Dr. Eduardo Salas, a team is two or more people working interdependently to accomplish a shared, valued goal. Interdependently means that no single member has the required skills or knowledge, so they must work together. They all have the same goal for which they are willing to give their time and effort, creating a shared value for the team. In contrast, groups are made up individuals who may not work interdependently, and groups may not share or value the same goal.

Teams also have some shared beliefs. They believe that teamwork is important, they want to be on the team, and they believe they have the skills and knowledge to be successful. They also trust and respect each other. Ultimately, team members support one another. Let's discuss the supporting behaviors that good teams perform in more detail. According to Team Dimensional Training, good teams support each other (1) by pointing out or correcting errors, and (2) by offering, requesting, and accepting backup. Supporting behaviors help teams ensure high-reliability operations in high-risk environments. Teams work in complex, ambiguous situations, plagued by threats, and prone to errors. Threats are events that happen externally to the team. In aviation, bad weather is a threat. Errors are events that happen internally to the team. Think of mistakes, lapses, and slips.

"Old school" safety experts believed errors occur when people lack training, motivation, or attention. People are "deficient" and that is why errors happen. But research has noticed that if different people were put in the same situation and they make the same errors, then the problem is not in the people but in the situation. So "new school" safety focuses more on fixing the situation, since providing more training, offering awards, or threatening to punish will NOT reduce errors.

Ideally you could improve the situation by making parts that cannot be installed wrong, or using displays that promote situation awareness and are associative to the desired action. But that is done by the organization days, weeks, or even years before the team starts their tasks. When the team starts, they have what they have, and all too often that is error-prone hardware, software, and procedures. They are left to discover supporting behaviors to help them mitigate.

The key to mitigating with supporting behaviors is aligning team member's mindset regarding errors. If you believe making an error is not a personal deficiency, then your ego does not get in the way. It is not a personal affront if someone points out an error you made. Both you and the person pointing out the error realize that you were "set up" by the situation. If an error isn't your fault, then you and the entire team can work together to correct the error by requesting or accepting backup behavior. For example, you might say, "I am about to start an error-prone procedure so look over my shoulder to make sure I don't screw up." Another example is a briefing like, "I might make a mistake, but you back me up and I will back you up." Such supporting behaviors work best when the culture is not about assessing blame, there is a low authority gradient (the difference in authority, experience, and status between the two people), and team members are cross-trained or perform similar tasks. Think of an airline crew. Airlines have worked hard to improve their culture and reduce the authority gradient. Also, both the captain and copilot alternate between who flies the plane or who monitors for safe operations. It is easy for the one monitoring to point out errors and offer backup assistance to the one doing the flying. Use of good supporting behaviors is one reason why airline accidents are so rare and flying is so safe.

But how does a team with highly differentiated knowledge and skills still support each other? How do you support your teammates even when you do not know exactly what s/he is doing? Admittedly this kind of support is more indirect and subtle. Instead of looking for actual errors or backing up someone by helping them do their job, the support is more psychological or emotional:

➤ "Hey, you look tired. How about I get you a cup of coffee?"

➢ "You looked stressed. What can I do to give you a few seconds to breathe?"
➢ "You are starting a tough procedure, where I know previous people made errors. What has been done to prevent, avoid, or mitigate errors for you? What could I do?"

TIP 16. TAKE YOUR TEAM'S EFFECTIVENESS TEMPERATURE

The emotional currents of a team are great indicators of team effectiveness, like thermometers are of our health. What kind of emotions does your team exhibit in the following seven (7) areas? If your team is running "cold" in any area, then the time is right for some team development assistance.

1) **Satisfaction with Leadership:** Team members feel the leader is a resource for support and coaching. The team perceives that the leader helps acquiring tools, equipment, information, and skills. The team feels that the leader helps identify, prioritize, and coordinate goals for the team—and keeps and disseminates the big picture for the team.

2) **Trust:** Team members trust each other and the leader to support them. Negative politics, gossip, and detrimental humor do not occur between team members. Team members are willing and able to share constructive criticism openly.

3) **Respect:** Each team member knows and values the others' perspectives, expertise, capabilities, and contributions.

4) **Cohesion:** The team can articulate a common purpose and/or set of goals. Team members prefer to work together. Team members speak in terms of "we" and "our team."

5) **Confidence in Complementary Skills:** Each team member contributes a necessary skill set. One member may have more project management skills, while another has more budgeting skills, and yet another has more technical writing skills. In a problem-solving session, a solution is suggested by one member, refined by another, challenged by a third, refined by another, and so forth until the team has developed the best workable solution.

6) **Open Communication, Communication is direct:** Team members do not need to choose words carefully when talking within the team. Team members are not afraid to speak their minds, admit mistakes, clarify roles, or propose new ideas. The team communicates frequently via several modes of communication.

7) **Lack of Selfishness:** Team members share credit and promote the goals and accomplishments of the team with outsiders. What is best for the team comes up in conversations consistently. Team members share the undesirable and desirable tasks equally.

Tip 17. Teamwork takes training

Managing or reducing uncertainties and their associated risks is the primary purpose of many teams' existence. As a consequence, teamwork training should enable your team to accomplish this purpose.

In 2002, then Secretary of Defense, Donald Rumsfeld, answered a question with "... as we know, there are known knowns; there are things that we know that we know. We also know there are known unknowns; that is to say we know there are some things we do not know. But there are also unknown unknowns, the ones we don't know we don't know."

We translate that into "Rumsfeld's Square," while adding another category: "unknown knowns" or tacit, previously inert, or emergent knowledge.

Known Knowns	Known Unknowns
Things we know we know	Things we know we don't know
Unknown Knowns	Unknown Unknowns
Things we don't know we know	Things that we don't know we don't know

Teamwork skills, like those taught through Minerva's Teamwork Training, or the military/aviation's Crew Resource Management (CRM), or healthcare's TeamSTEPPS, focus on increasing the numbers of knowns and managing the unknowns' impact on team performance. More specifically, the goals of teamwork skills training are to teach teams how to:

1) **Determine the number of Known Knowns**
   Each member of the team has unique knowledge, specific to his/her position and experience. This means basically each team member contributes what s/he knows, but not just a "data dump" of everything s/he knows. This requires every team member to know who needs what information and when. So, it is "I know this, and I realize that you need to know it now."

2) **Turn Unknown Knowns into emergent knowledge**
   This can happen in two ways. The first way is to combine the limited bits of information from two or more team members into a relevant whole understanding. An example from NASA is that one flight controller sees the control system is having unexpected difficulty maintaining the vehicle's attitude. Another flight controller sees a possible air leak but can't tell if it is external or internal. Neither can figure it out singly, but together they figure out that a real external leak is providing an unwanted

torque of the vehicle. This requires turning individual situation awareness into team situation awareness.

A second way is through syncing mental models. A mental model is how you believe something works. No matter how smart or experienced you are, everyone has holes and errors in their mental models. The good news with teams is the holes in your mental model are not holes in mine. Together we can develop a mental model that is more correct and more complete. This requires conflict management, specifically mental model conflict management.

3) **Define Known Unknowns to Make them Known Knowns**

Sometimes we can change Unknowns to Knowns by doing an analysis, running a simulation, doing some research, or calling an expert. Sometimes we have to settle for making Unknowns just a little more Known and agree on some parameters for working flexibly. One way to do that is making contingency plans with all the proper information requirements and triggers. For example, when we can't be sure if, when, or how hardware will fail but failures have happened in the past, then we may plan ahead of time, as a team, that if hardware does fail, we will save the system first and then hold a meeting to determine what to do next. A second way is by pre-finding and testing errors. We may not know what errors we might make, but we know we will make some. The required team skill is supporting behaviors where team members back each other up in complex, error-prone, or high workload/distraction situations.

4) **Adapt when an Unknown Unknown suddenly materializes**

An Unknown Unknown can't be anticipated. It is beyond anything we expected from our training and experience. A required team skill is adapting. It could be as little as saying, "tell me if you see ANYTHING out of the norm, no matter how small. We will then discuss it as a team to figure out what is happening and what we should do.

To summarize, successful teamwork skills training allows the team to say:

➢ We have a plan to handle what we think will happen (handling Known Knowns and Unknown Knowns).
➢ We have contingency plans to handle what we think might happen (handling Known Unknowns).
➢ We have a process and skills to handle surprises (handling Unknown Unknowns).

If your team training is not training you to do all this, then your training is inadequate. If you are unsure if your training is adequate or you are sure your training falls short, then your first steps should be a training needs analysis and a review and evaluation of your training's utility in your teamwork context. If you don't train teamwork skills, but depend on teams to manage work projects, then your first step should be procuring or creating behavior-based teamwork skills training.

Tip 18. Use S.T.A.R. Moments to Avert Disasters

The S.T.A.R. (Stop, Think, Act, Review) moment is the time-out that stands between your team and a nuclear disaster. During our work with teams in extreme environments doing experiential teamwork skills training, we realized that many teams struggle to get every team member on the same page. Starting the decision-making process to address a crisis with just one ear halfway open to the rest of the team is a great way to kill everyone. Unfortunately, as humans, we're naturally anxious and we tend to believe we should be able to multitask—especially in a crisis—which research shows is impossible.

When things are on fire, the best performing teams call for a pause and force everyone to stop multitasking. This allows everyone space to use both ears and their entire brains to engage in a more efficient group decision-making process. As a high-performing team, we at Minerva do this by literally saying, "Wait, STAR moment." This causes everyone in the room to immediately realize that one of us has recognized a critical threat or opportunity. As a team, we then know that the next few minutes will be spent on these steps:

1) **Stop.** We face each other and stop responding to any stimuli outside of our other team members (i.e. phones go unanswered). First, how much time do we have to think about this? Is it a safety issue? Cost issue? Do we need to do something to buy ourselves time to think before acting? We set a deadline for our pause. By default, we go for five minutes immediately.

2) **Think.** The person calling for the STAR moment states the concern. Why is it a concern? What do we think is the biggest potential impact to our team, mission, system, goal? The person calling the STAR is also tasked with making a recommendation. The rest of the team is responsible for vetting that recommendation.

3) **Plan to Act.** Once we all consent to a workable recommendation, we talk about who will implement what and when. We assign responsibilities, if not tasks, to specific team members and set deadlines.

4) **Review.** Finally, we talk about how we will know that our plan is working. We set up metrics and check-points. Sometimes this is as simple as saying we will see if anyone is pulling their hair out tomorrow morning. We don't go back to work until everyone understands how we'll handle the threat or opportunity as a team.

STAR moments create feelings of competence among individual team members and increase team members' confidence in leadership. STAR moments prompt knowledge sharing and promote a climate of psychological safety, because team members are not afraid to give leaders the actionable information necessary to fix or avoid errors. There is a bit of the chicken and the egg scenario going on here; strong teams use STAR moments; STAR moments make teams even stronger. The first step is to start leveraging STAR moments as a team. If you can't figure out how to apply it in your work context right away, then even using STAR moments during training events will help. Your team will learn the mechanics of effective teamwork together, enough to become a stronger team.

TIP 19. DO 5 THINGS ALL GREAT TEAMS DO

1) Have team skills training.
   Research Says...Team skills training, cross training, and simulation-based team training will help team members learn teamworking skills and effectively enhance team performance (Klein et al., 2005).
2) Know what your teammates know and don't know.
   Research says...Positional Modeling (showing each team member what every position on the team does and why) improves team performance (Marks, Sabella, Burke, & Zaccaro, 2002).
3) Practice-guided team self-correction.
   Research says...Teams whose debriefs were led by an expert, who focused on the right processes for making decisions across different circumstances, outperformed teams who led their own debriefs and spent too much time focused on what decisions were made right in the present circumstances (Smith-Jentsch et al., 2008).
4) Discuss progress and obstacles regularly.
   Research says...Talking about what worked and didn't work throughout and after project completion, in both formal and informal settings,

leads team members to do more planning, collaborative problem solving, and task coordination on subsequent projects (Ellis et al., 2005).

5) Use individual and team feedback well.

Research says...Individual feedback results in higher individual performance at the expense of the team performance (and vice versa), while individual and team feedback provided together prevents either performance from being maximized (DeShon, 2004). So, provide team feedback to the entire team in public if team performance is the goal (don't do individual feedback) or provide individualized feedback privately to each team member if individual performance is the goal (and don't do team feedback). All in one or two for one does not work.

Tip 20. Do 5 more things really great teams do

1) Use Situational Leaders.
   Research says...Team members expect the leader to direct the task and to develop team members (usually by coaching), so it works better when the smartest person is the leader of that task, not necessarily the designated leader (Burke et al., 2007).

2) Share metacognition.
   Research says...Experts know what strategies they use to learn or think about a problem and can adjust these strategies as needed; this is metacognition. Teaching and encouraging team members to engage in metacognition increases the team's overall expertise (Day, Gronn, & Salas, 2004).

3) Encourage team adaptability.
   Research says...Adaptability is the ability to change performance processes in response to the environment. Experts are good at this because they know how to facilitate others through these phases of adaptation too (Salas, Rosen, Burke, & Goodwin, 2008).

4) Get stress exposure through training before experiencing it on the job.

    Research says...When training familiarizes trainees with environmental stressors, and builds trainees' confidence in their ability to perform in uncertain and stressful conditions, then such training diminishes the impact of stress on the quality of that team's decisions (Paris, Salas, & Cannon-Bowers, 2000).

5) Use team training developed by team leaders and context experts.

    Research says...Training developed and implemented by leaders and task experts survives longer, enjoys better student transfer of learning, and results in bigger payoffs for the organization (Adelsberg & Trolley, 1999).

Tip 21. Honor the Foremost High-Performance Teamwork Skill

You have an important task that needs to be done, and it can't be done by one person. You will need a team. You have a group of individuals of different occupations and with different levels of experience and training. Most have never worked together, and some have little experience with teamwork.

How do you turn that group into a High-Performance Team, a team that will not only get the job done, but get it done effectively, efficiently, and safely?

One of the first things you will need to do is "get them on the same page." You want them to have a shared understanding of the task and what needs to be done, the environment in which they will work, and how they will operate as a team. Let's cover developing a shared understanding of task, environment, and team separately.

The easiest shared understanding is *task*. You probably already do a good job explaining the task, but there may be areas for improvement. You could start with, "Team, today we are going to activate a new piece of equipment," or design something or fix something. If your team has done that task before, especially recently and well, you might think developing a shared understanding is not necessary. That depends. Is this the same or are there subtle changes that might be the difference between success and failure, or safe and unsafe? Or maybe you aren't sure if the team was successful because they were good or were just lucky. If you are worried about good versus lucky, and you have a specific way or process you want them to follow, make sure they understand the process. Also explain why following the process is important to them and to getting the task done properly.

The discussion could be as simple as, "Last time we had a lot of waste and we almost got a few people hurt. So, this time we are going to ...," and say it aloud. Once the team knows the right way to do the task, they need to know what success looks like: how they can tell if things are going well. An example is, "We should have the first milestone done by tomorrow," or "The temperature (or pressure or ...) should never reach X." If everything goes as expected, first milestone by tomorrow or parameters within limits, the team knows they should continue. If things are not going as planned, they know that something might be wrong and that they need to tell you. Your contingency planning depends on the task but might be as little as, "If we miss the first milestone, let's relook at our plan and process," or "If we violate a limit, let's stop and investigate." By the end of the task discussion, all the team members know what you want done and how, how to tell whether the task is going as planned or not, and what to do if it isn't.

The next shared understanding is ***environment***, or the surroundings in which you are doing the task. Maybe you have been building houses, but this is the first one on clay soil or under new regulations; or instead of 3 weeks to do it, you will have only 2; or your team is a little tired or has new team members. In the airline world, this is a discussion of threats and errors. Threats are something that can happen to you outside your control. Bad weather is a common example of a threat. You can't control the weather, but you will have to react if the weather turns bad. Another common threat is an equipment failure. Most threats are specific to your environment, but you know the most likely ones. You can discuss them with your team with as little as, "If we get lightning within 5 miles, we stop all outside work," or "If the pump fails, we will stop until we can get the back-up going." Errors are things that you do to yourself by doing something you weren't supposed to or not doing something you were. You know the most likely errors so tell the team. Examples might be, "Remember last time we did …," or "We are going to be rushed (or tired), so everyone needs to…."

The last shared understanding is ***team***, or how you expect the team to operate. This is where most teams come up short: they had different thoughts on how they should work with each other. If you have ever heard, "I assumed you were …," or much worse, "Speak when spoken to," then you have team issues and should take advantage of team skills training as quickly as possible.

TIP 22. PAY ATTENTION TO TEAM COMMUNICATION BASICS

You are doing a review of your team's last project. One of the problems mentioned was poor communication. What is that? How are you going to fix it?

Communication is the passing of information from one person to another. It can be verbal (a conversation or radio message), written (an email or a form), visual (body language or hand signal) or even touch (a pat on the shoulder). Good communication requires responsibilities for the sender, the one initiating the flow of information, and the receiver, the one receiving the information. The reason that communication is usually the most common cited team deficiency is because communication is observable. Even experienced instructors sometimes confuse what is observable with the skill. Let me explain with an example:

We agree that I am supposed to email you which step to start on. Let's assume that the correct step to start on is Step 7. Is communication the observable issue if:

1) I email you to start Step 8? (That is the wrong information but delivered clearly and concisely and in the right format.)
2) Instead of an email, from across the room, I show you seven fingers and mouth "Step 7"? (That is the

right information delivered clearly and concisely but not in the format we agreed.)

3) I email you, "I finished Step 6, you're next"? (That is the right information in the right format, but I use ambiguous terms.)

My contention is that communication is an issue in Number 2 (wrong format) and Number 3 (what I call "style") but not in Number 1. I consider Number 1 a Situation Awareness issue. In Number 1, I don't know what the right answer is, and no amount of communication training can help that. Communication training can help with Numbers 2 and 3.

Let's deal with communication format issues first. Without format, the sender doesn't know what information to pass or how to package the information for best understanding. Without format, the receiver is left guessing what information is coming and how it is arranged. A good format helps the sender decide what information to pass and in what order. A good format helps the receiver quickly process the information. In NASA's International Space Station's Mission Control Center, flight controllers pass information on equipment failures in a Failure-Impact-Workaround (FIW) format: what failed, how does that failure affect the system, vehicle, and mission, and what they think should be done to fix or remediate the failure. In healthcare, some organizations use the Situation-Background-Assessment-Recommendation (SBAR) format: here is what is happening, the context, what it means and what they think the team should do. In summary, if you tell me what I expect in the manner I expect to hear it, I will understand you more quickly, better, and with less mental effort.

Now let's address what I call "style." Style is the list of adverbs and adjectives that most people think about when they think about good communication. Good communication should be timely, accurate, clear, concise, confident, consistent, professional, proactive, objective, and tailored. Although each adjective or adverb could profit from its own explanation, this last one is especially important for ensuring that active listening is possible. Each communication must be tailored to the experience and training of the listener. If you have a listener who is brand new to the job and to you, your message must be a lot different than if your listener is highly experienced and has worked with you for a long time.

Finally, let's talk a little about the receiver's responsibility: to be an active listener. I define an active listener as one who is making a deliberate effort to understand the message the sender is sending. Active listening is **<u>NOT</u>** anticipatory listening (listening for what you expect to hear), defensive listening (listening to argue), dismissive listening (half listening because you don't think that the information is important), or passive listening (listening but no processing). You can tell when people are being active listeners when they say such things as, "rephrasing in my own words, you mean…," or "if I understand you correctly, you need…."

I'd like to close by describing one method many organizations use to ensure good communication, known as the "three-way communication" or "closed loop communication" method. The method is that the first person communicates information, then the second person repeats what s/he thinks the first person communicated, then the first person confirms the second person properly understood.

An example:
Joe: "Jane, I need you to open the flow control all the way."
Jane: "You want me to turn the flow control valve all the way counter-clockwise."
Joe: "Correct, I want you turn the flow control valve all the way counter-clockwise to open it now."

Three-way communication requires both people to use the right format and right style, and then to actively listen to each other.

Tip 23. Get your team to see the big picture

As a team leader, you want everyone on your team to have "the Big Picture" and know what is going on around them. What you want is for each member of your team to have good Situation Awareness (SA). The most referenced definition of SA is by Dr. Mica Endsley:

"...The perception of elements in the environment within a volume of time and space, the comprehension of their meaning, and the projection of their status in the near future."

Having good individual SA requires each team member to perceive what is going on around him or her, and comprehend what that means now and in the near future. Let's start with the comprehending portion first, because that is how high-performance teams start.

Before beginning their shift/next event:

- ➢ The team discusses what should and might happen, and how that affects their ability to perform that task.
- ➢ They discuss what they want to do and what the expected results would look like.

➢ They discuss what might go wrong either due to external factors (threats) or internal factors (errors), what each threat and error might look like, and what would be the results of each threat or error, until the team has audibly built a shared understanding about what to watch out for during task performance.

By the end of the discussion, the team would know what they should be perceiving and comprehending, and what should and might happen now and in the future.

During the shift or task, you want everyone on your team noticing what is or is not happening. This covers the perception portion of SA: seeing, hearing, feeling, tasting, or smelling what is going on around you. There are two main reasons why people fail to perceive well enough to support a team's performance. The first is "environmental," meaning it was too hot, or too cold, or too dark, or too bright, or too noisy, or too whatever for your team member to perceive properly. Or maybe the team member didn't have the right information, or the information is mixed up with too much extraneous data for anyone to pick it out, or it was too ambiguous. The second reason that someone didn't perceive properly is because s/he was too busy doing something else, either due to workload or distractions. It turns out the easiest and best way to improve chances of perceiving properly is managing workload and distractions.

Beyond perceiving something, the team member must realize if the data is or is not what was expected. Why would someone not understand that something is wrong?

The first reason is again workload or distractions. The team member did not have the time or mental resources to think about it (i.e., to comprehend). If you hear, "If I had a second to think about it, I would have figured it out," you have a workload/distraction problem. Or it might be a related multi-tasking problem, where people are jumping between tasks. There is an "SA tax" every time someone jumps back to a task, a few seconds when the person must rebuild their SA to where they were, what was happening, and what it meant. If they don't have the time to rebuild that SA, errors are very possible. Managing workload, distractions, and multi-tasking is again the easiest way to improve your SA. The second reason is due to lack of training or experience; that is, the team member didn't know that something was wrong, or couldn't comprehend or project its impact.

Finally, about what areas does the team need to have SA? If you were an airline captain, it is not enough to perceive high engine temperature, and comprehend and project a future engine failure. I call that Subsystem SA. You also must comprehend how that will affect the airplane (System SA), your ability to get to Seattle (Mission SA) while flying over the Rocky Mountains (Environment SA) with an inexperienced co-pilot (Team SA). Regardless of what you call the various terms, it is important to note that to have good overall SA, you and your team are required to perceive, comprehend, and project over this wider, nested range of information. This is usually accomplished by using what is called a scan pattern that you and your team develop together. For example, you may decide to check your Subsystem SA on the tenth minute of every hour, your

System SA every 3o minutes, your Team SA every shift change, and your Mission SA every week. Keeping the requirements of both perceiving and comprehending in mind will help you get your team to see the big picture.

Tip 24. When failure is not an option, rely on experiential training

Roughly 70% of technical project failures are due to human errors. A large portion of these errors could have been avoided altogether, or at least corrected in enough time to prevent failure, if every team member minimally understood how to work as a situational leader and supportive follower. In other words, when such failures are not a good option for your organization, it pays to train team leadership like an astronaut.

Astronauts know that the best way to learn how to work in teams is through experiential teamwork and leadership training. Completing the training as a team is best of all, but even participating in such training of teamwork and leadership skills as an individual significantly improves both individual and team performance.

Such training does NOT have to be based on expensive high-fidelity or technical simulations to be effective either. Turns out that the important bits are the experiential and behavioral parts. Training must allow participants to practice applying leadership behaviors in an experience that requires teamwork to survive and succeed.

Additionally, the threat of failure is a powerful learning motivator even if it's just failing to win a game. There are also added benefits in that high-performing (high-potential) employees who engage in such training gain confidence in their leadership abilities and report increases in their engagement with the work. They increase their commitment to their organizations, so teamwork leadership training can help you retain your best talent. Leaders who practice in experiential training also learn how to more effectively manage the deep-level diversity issues (like differences in values, perspectives, and cultures) that really impact a team's performance. The bottom line is that when team leadership failure is not an option for your organization, then investing in simple, yet engaging, experiential teamwork and leadership training is a wise way to gain a return on investment.

TIP 25. CULTIVATE GOOD TEAM CONFLICT

Your team will have conflicts. Conflicts, if handled properly, will give your team new insights; if handled improperly they could lead to a poor decision.

Team conflict due to differences in mental models, values, approaches, and culture are especially important, assuming two key things. First, your team meets Dr. Eduardo Salas' definition of a "team," that is, two or more people working interdependently to accomplish a **shared** and **valued** goal. This allows me to not consider team members who are working their own personal or organizational agendas. Second, your people are professionals who can temporarily put aside personal differences.

Let's start with conflicts due to different mental models. Simply put, mental models are how you believe something works. You have a mental model on how a car works. Mine is turn-key-car-go. Depending on your knowledge, experience, and need, your mental model of a car may be very different than that of a NASCAR driver or a mechanic or an automotive engineer. That is okay if your mental model meets your needs. But say you are the team leader of a project to design a new feature for a car, and your team members are me, a NASCAR driver, a mechanic, and a design engineer. As we discuss how to design the new feature, there will be differences in opinion, many due to differences in how we think a car works. Because my mental model is so different from the others, I often ask questions or make suggestions that don't make sense to you or the rest of the team. As a leader, you could just ignore my questions and suggestions, just like many team leaders ignore inputs from "the rookie" or "that guy who doesn't have a clue." If you do so, you may imperil your project. Every mental model, no matter how much experience and training you and the other team members have, has "holes." "Holes" are where your mental model is inaccurate or incomplete. One of the main advantages of teams is that we have those different mental models. Most importantly, the holes in my mental model do not line up with the holes in yours. In other words, I know something that you don't, and vice versa. With enough team members with different mental models, a team can hope to minimize holes. So as team leader, you must decide if my mental model is so bad that it adds no value, or is it possible that I am exposing a hole in the rest of the team's mental model? How you decide to handle my "that's not how I thought it worked" or "that doesn't make sense to me" may determine how complete a team mental model you have. Many an accident has been averted when the leader asked, "the rookie" what s/he meant by that comment (e.g., is it supposed to do that?), and then deliberately tried to modify his/her mental model based on that comment.

Even if the team has a common or at least complementary mental model, there still will be conflict.

One cause is differences in what I call "values." For example: how much risk I am willing to take to achieve our goal versus the risk with which you are comfortable. You see this conflict a lot in discussions between operations and safety people. You also see differences in values between Sales, Marketing, Manufacturing, and Engineering departments. They value different aspects of the business and hence have different ideas about what should be most important.

Yet another reason for conflict is a difference in organizational approach or differences in the 4 Ps (Philosophy, Policies, Processes, and Practices), or the "that is (not) how we do it" debates. A related conflict is culture. I define culture as a way of thinking specific to a group of people. Culture can restrict what they think about, how they think about it, and what they are willing to do. Most people think in terms of national cultures (e.g., Americans versus Japanese), but there are others: professional (engineers versus scientists), organizational (Engineering versus Sales), and even generational (Baby Boomers versus Millennials) and gender (men versus women).

How your team handles differences in mental models, values, approach, and culture will determine its success—both in terms of performance and resilience. It is worth remembering that the leader sets the team's conflict discussion tone, and every team member contributes to the group's openness when it comes to managing conflict.

TIP 26. REMEMBER THAT ELIMINATING WRONGS DOESN'T HELP YOU WIN

You'll never win when you only debrief what went wrong. This is like trying to coach a basketball team by only telling them what not to do. If you want to win more as a team at work, then debrief every major project (e.g., project completion, grant application, board meeting, policy, or system implementation) as a team by talking about: (1) What did we do well that we should try again in similar situations? and (2) What didn't go as well as we hoped and what do we want to try doing differently next time?

Use the following facilitated debriefing tactics gleaned from research to make your debriefs even more likely to help you win:

➢ **Address each other directly and as a team.** Your ability to continue to learn and self-correct your team depends on establishing a safe learning climate. To do this, you will need to remember that titles and status are irrelevant during debriefs and that you must participate and encourage others to do so.

> **Analyze why situations happened.** Think about what events contributed to the final outcome and what behaviors influenced those events. Offer behavioral examples for discussion by the team.

> **Discuss how you were affected by others' actions.** What did they do that helped you? What information or help do you wish you were given by others?

> **Discuss what you were thinking.** Explain your rationale for doing or not doing something. What was your understanding of what was happening at the time and how was that accurate and inaccurate?

> **Discuss what went well.** What did the team do right that it should keep doing?

> **Discuss what could be improved and how.** What could be done differently to make teamwork easier in similar situations next time?

> **Discuss what factors enabled or impeded your success.** What obstacles to teamwork were inherent in the situation and how could the team work around them in the future? What situational factors contributed to the team's success and how could the team leverage these factors in similar future situations? What tools help you do good teamwork?

> **Discuss how to apply what you learned to your job.** Concentrate on finding two to three new things you can do or tools you can use to ensure you work well on teams tomorrow in any situation.

TIP 27. KNOW IF YOUR TEAM IS MAKING GOOD DECISIONS

How can you tell if your team is making good decisions? One way is to check if they behave like a team making good decisions should. What are those behaviors?

Albert Einstein said, "If I had an hour to solve a problem and my life depended on the solution, I would spend the first 55 minutes determining the proper question to ask, for once I know the proper question, I could solve the problem in less than five minutes." This quote emphasizes that the first and possibly most important step in decision making is situation assessment.

Research confirms Einstein's statement that teams that make good decisions treat decision making as a two-step process. First, they make sure that they understand the situation, i.e., do a good situation assessment. Only after they understand the situation do they move to the second step: selecting a course of action.

The first step is to look for more information and cues. When there is complexity, or incomplete, unreliable, or conflicting data, experienced people will try to make sense of the data by building a "story" that explains how they got into the situation. Stories use the data from the past and present, along with experience, to "fill in some

82

blanks" to develop a logical flow of how the situation got where it is today. Stories allow the team to check for inconsistencies, to determine what additional data to look for, and to give a context to make projections into the future. If the first story is too full of inconsistencies, or additional data does not confirm it, or future projections are wrong, then another story may better fit the data. An example might be for a sudden loss of power. One "story" is a power failure, but an alternative "story" might be that someone bumped the power switch. The team then looks for additional cues that would help them eliminate alternative stories.

The team also must look at critical factors that define the problem or constrain any possible solution. What are the factors that the team will use to select the course of action? The critical circumstances may be organizational constraints, or which team members are available, or time, or cost. If you only have an hour before something bad happens (i.e., a critical factor), don't look at options that take a day to implement. **The selected course of action must satisfy the critical factors.**

Good decision makers are habitually better at perceiving and recognizing capabilities and limitations. Poor decision makers tend to underestimate risk, and over-estimate their skill. **Good teams look at what threats or errors might cause them to have problems.** They also look at history; if all previous teams took two days to do this task, why do they believe they can get it done in six hours? **Poor decision makers base current decisions on previous successes or failures.** They do not consider if previous successes were due to just being lucky, or if a previous failure was due to being unlucky.

Finally, good decision makers also realize that they might be making bad assumptions. To compensate, they determine what information is required to prove that they are wrong. By specifically looking for information that would prove them wrong, they can better determine if their situation assessment is correct. Another way is to get outsiders, or fresh eyes, to review the team's situation assessment. Because they were not part of the original situation assessment, the outsiders may not have the same assumptions. An outsider might catch something the team missed. If outsiders are not available, then the team could try a "Devil's Advocate," someone on the team who is tasked to challenge the team's assessment. This check of the team's situation assessment is the hallmark of good decision makers. After the team does a sound situation assessment, then and only then, should they progress to deciding a course of action.

Tip 28. Respond well to unexpected events

You may have started to hear the term "VUCA environments" to describe the ever-changing, production-focused, and technology-driven work environment that organizations find themselves in today. (Even the acronym is a little intimidating!)

VUCA stands for volatile, uncertain, complex, and ambiguous. Many agree current work environments continue to take on more of these characteristics as organizations struggle to keep up with industry, their competitors, and their customers' needs. At a personal level, you may be able to relate as well. Are you concerned with how to keep up with the latest technology (knowing which tools are worth your investment of time)? Do you feel that established best practices may not be working in your team's workflows or projects? Are you concerned with how to address complex issues (e.g., marketing on a global level or handling a multi-level project with constantly moving parts) as an effective leader in your organization?

Bechky and Okhuysen (2011) describe how bricolage teams handle these very situations. The term "bricolage" is defined as "construction achieved by using whatever comes to hand." Organizations that handle VUCA environments well, handle bricolage well. In fact, researchers have found that when surprises disrupt expectations, improvisational organizational action leads to learning, problem solving, and change. In other words, organizations that can improvise (bricolage) are more resilient and are able to take action that helps them learn, problem solve, and change.

To increase your team's ability to bricolage:

Build cross-member expertise–this will improve your resource capacity for bricolaging (e.g., if Joe knows what Susan does, when a crisis happens he can step in and help, identify other possible solutions, etc.).

Share task knowledge–it's important for other members within the team to effectively communicate and share their knowledge of a specific task or project. Leaders should set time for this at the beginning of a project or task, and then identify specific communication points along the project timeline. This will re-engage the team and check for shared task knowledge and understanding.

Set expectations for workflow—even when a team is familiar with a project, workflow, or task (or at least they think they are), it's important to set expectations of how things are expected to play out. Teams should communicate these expectations together at the beginning of the project and on a consistent basis throughout the duration of the project. When things do go awry, which they will, the team already has a mechanism in place to regroup and set expectations for how they plan to proceed.

The study referenced is:

Becky, B.A & Okhuysen, G.O. (2011). Expecting the unexpected? How SWAT officers and film crews handle surprises. *Academy of Management Journal*, 54(2), 239-261.

SECTION THREE: PROFESSIONAL DEVELOPMENT

TIP 29. HAVE A POINT

Research suggests humans aren't great predictors of the future. And we aren't good at this because we use our current surroundings and past experiences to predict what we guestimate the future will hold. But these cues turn out not to be very good indicators when considering the rapid pace of change we find ourselves in today. And this makes sense—just think of smart phones as an example. You couldn't have accounted for how the development of smart phones has singularly changed how you interact with people or how you get your work done every single day.

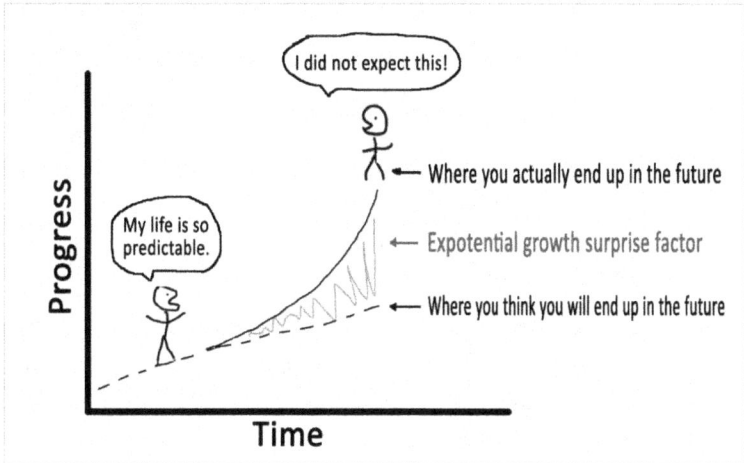

We may not be able to predict our own futures well because we can't control for our surroundings and how they will change. BUT we can use goal-setting theory to create SMART goals to control our own behavior and what we set out to accomplish. So really, the point is to spend the time to have an endpoint in mind. Spend time contemplating your career or personal path, where you are headed, and what it will take to get there. Spend the time setting goals, and maybe reaching the goal is not really that important (because you won't be able to correctly guess what that will look like anyway). Maybe what really counts, as with most things, is the time invested going through the process of contemplating those big questions (What do I want from my career? What do I want to accomplish?), setting a direction to define that path forward, and taking those steps to achieve those goals.

TIP 30. LEVERAGE SMART GOAL-SETTING

Goal Setting Theory is a well validated theory from organizational psychologists Edwin Locke and Gary Latham that specifically says for goals to be achievable, they need to be SMART:

➢ **Specific**—"I want to lose 10 pounds."
➢ **Measurable**—"I'm going to weigh myself every Friday."
➢ **Achievable**—"I actually have 10 pounds that I can actually lose without putting my health at risk."
➢ **Realistic**—"I'm trying to lose 5% of my body weight, not 45%."
➢ **Time-bound**—"I project that I'll lose 10 pounds in 3 months."

Multiple researchers have published papers and meta-analyses backing up these concepts, which means that **setting goals in a specific way increases your chance of achieving them.** Of course, this isn't just work-specific, it's any goal in any situation.

TIP 31. PRIORITIZE ACTIONS BY EFFORT AND IMPACT

The Action Priority Matrix (Figure 1) is a simple diagramming technique from executive coaching that helps you choose which activities to prioritize, and which ones you should drop when the pressure is greatest, if you want to make the most of your time and opportunities. It's useful because most of us have many more activities on our "wish lists"—whether these are bright ideas to pursue, exciting opportunities, or interesting possibilities—than we have time available. By choosing activities intelligently, you can make the very most of your time and opportunities.

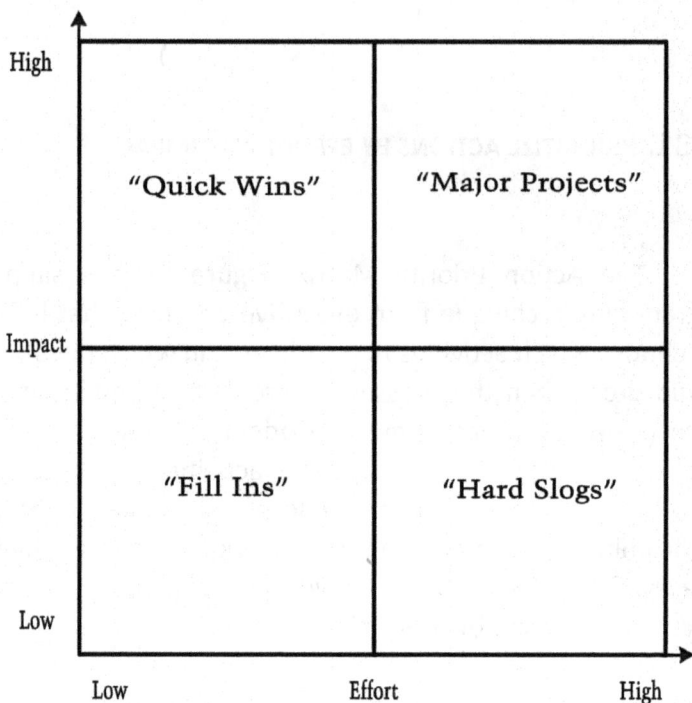

How to Use the Tool:

The principle behind using the tool is that you score each activity you want to complete on two scales—firstly on the impact the activity will have, and secondly on the effort involved. By plotting each activity on the Action Priority Matrix using these scores, you can quickly see the projects that give you the greatest returns on your efforts, and adopt the most appropriate approach for that type of activity:

1) **Quick Wins** (High Impact, Low Effort): These are the most attractive projects, giving you a good return for relatively little effort. Focus on these as much as you can.

2) **Major Projects** (High Impact, High Effort): While these give good returns, they take a long time to complete—meaning that one "Major Project" can crowd out many "Quick Wins." If you're engaging in major projects, make sure that you complete them quickly and efficiently and that you disengage your effort as soon as you can.

3) **Fill Ins** (Low Impact, Low Effort): Don't worry too much about doing these—if you've got spare time, do them, but drop them if something better comes along.

4) **Hard Slogs** (Low Impact, High Effort): Avoid these. Not only do they give low returns, they crowd out time which would be better used elsewhere.

A good rule of thumb for executive leaders is to make sure eighty percent of your time is spent on quick wins. Major projects should be delegated to high-potential employees as responsibilities (i.e., not tasks). Also, projects more than six months out should be put in an "icebox" list that you review (e.g., once a week/month). A project can move from the icebox to your priority matrix when they are less than 6 months out, when you have extra room/time among your priorities, or when your operating context makes an icebox project due sooner than expected. A final word of caution, don't exceed more than 8 items per category in the matrix during any six-month period. If you have more than 32 projects in your matrix this is a sign that you need to rebalance your workload into something you can reasonably expect to achieve as a human.

Tip 32. Use the Art of Getting Effective Feedback

What would receiving frequent, specific, high-quality feedback at work do for you? Adequate performance feedback is critical for ensuring that performance expectations are being met. In addition, when working to build new skills, high-quality feedback allows us to gauge how our efforts are coming across and what mid-course corrections need to be made to achieve important development goals. Yet, many people say that they don't get enough feedback at work or that the feedback they receive is not very helpful (e.g., "You are doing fine").

As a feedback recipient, there are things you can do to help ensure that the feedback you receive is valuable and can be leveraged to help you achieve your goals.

1) **Take the initiative and "prime the pump."** A desire for feedback is not always obvious, so actively request feedback from those in key settings with whom you interact. In addition, be specific about the type of feedback you'd like. Instead of saying, "Jane, can you give me some feedback about how I did on my presentation?" approach her before the presentation and say, "Jane, I'm working on

developing more persuasive and compelling rationale when expressing my ideas. Would you mind giving me some feedback on what I do well and less well in that area after Tuesday's presentation to the sales team?" This will help direct Jane to the information that is most pertinent to your situation and goals.

2) **Focus on listening and understanding.** When Jane communicates her feedback, give her your undivided attention. If you don't understand her comments, ask clarifying questions and request examples of what she saw. At the end of the conversation, summarize what you heard and ask her if you understood her points correctly.

3) **Resist the urge to explain.** Particularly when hearing feedback about behavior that came across differently from what was intended, it's tempting to explain our motives For example, I wasn't crossing my arms and legs during the meeting because I didn't like what Paul said. I was freezing and was trying to stay warm! Explaining behavior can come across as justification, excuses, or defensiveness. Consider carefully whether it's best to hold your thoughts or share your perspective when receiving feedback.

4) **Express appreciation.** Thank Jane for taking the time and effort to give you feedback. If you disagree with her message or suggestions, you can still say something like, "Thank you for sharing your

perspective. I will take your ideas under consideration."

5) **Set the stage for the future.** You will need additional feedback as you continue working toward your development goals and it may be appropriate to ask Jane for her comments at a later time. Think carefully about when and how to make future requests. For example, if you received a lot of constructive suggestions the last time you spoke to Jane, it may be best to demonstrate some progress to show that you have taken her comments seriously before asking for additional feedback from her.

Taking these actions will help you improve your performance, take some of the guess work out of development, and reach your goals more efficiently.

TIP 33. GIVE GOOD FEEDBACK

Why is it important to give effective feedback?

1) If you're a supervisor, manager, or business owner, then you already give feedback as part of your daily job—so you might as well do it really well.
2) Frequent feedback, positive and negative, contributes to employee satisfaction and productivity, and in turn, drives product and service quality.
3) Employees who get good feedback on a regular basis are happier with their managers, with their work, and stay in the job longer than those who get little to no feedback (in every industry and type of organization).

What does a manager get out of giving feedback (besides more work)?

1) Employees report fewer problems and engage in more helping behaviors that promote the business.

2) When employees are given good feedback, managers spend substantially less time dealing with employee performance issues and attendance problems.
3) Businesses that give employees feedback get significantly better customer service ratings and their employees suggest more innovations.
4) Leaders who are skilled at giving feedback get more promotions and raises (and faster) than those who do not know how to give good feedback to employees.

How do you know when it is effective?

It's concise—you can accomplish a lot by saying only a little. Also, employees actually ask for it.

Seven simple ground rules for giving good feedback.

1) **Be a coach.** All feedback is developmental or should be, so express interest in developing the employee by asking how it is best for you to share feedback with them and using the response to customize your approach.
2) **Be immediate.** Focus on behaviors that are happening right now, or very recently, since drawing connections too far in the past is confusing for both you and your employee.

3) **Be specific.** Cite observed behaviors as examples and give examples of specific behaviors that you expect or want to see now.

4) **Be explicit.** Don't give hints to preserve face and take a chance your message being missed. If you focus on behaviors only, and express confidence in an employee's ability to behaviorally succeed, then you will rarely offend while still providing useful feedback.

5) **Share responsibility.** Ask how you can help your employee succeed now. The responsibility for better and better performance belongs to both of you.

6) **Be supportive.** Admit that getting feedback is scary and hard, and express your intentions to make it useful—because you want everyone to have their best chance to succeed and be happy.

7) **Document it.** Notes not only help you justify or explain future employment decisions, they also help you remember what feedback worked or didn't work with each individual, and improve your own skill at giving feedback.

Tip 34. Keep practicing how you manage conflict

We may not like to engage in conflict, but we know from team research that conflict is a necessary part of working well. Efficient conflict resolution is a key teamwork skill. And, ineffective or unmanaged conflict is detrimental to the team and its performance. Effective conflict management creates a process for conflict to be resolved optimally and has demonstrable, positive effects for both the individual and the team. Research shows that properly managed conflict increases organizational learning by increasing the number of questions asked, and encourages people to challenge the status quo.

To manage conflict better on the job, remember these research-based pointers:

➢ Ask questions to understand the other person(s),
➢ Be prepared to compromise,
➢ Assume you do NOT have all the answers,
➢ And when you engage in the conflict, practice active listening (e.g., paraphrasing what the others have said to show that you have understood) and show

empathy (e.g., when speaking, start by acknowledging their feelings).

It also helps to take a moment to reflect on the conflict you may be experiencing at work or elsewhere right now. Jot down how you will approach that conflict by integrating the key points described above. Think about the other parties' point of view and make sure you fully understand it. Brainstorm possible compromises that might be acceptable to all parties, but don't assume your answers will be the right one.

TIP 35. ALWAYS PLAY YOUR PART IN MAINTAINING PSYCHOLOGICAL SAFETY

Whenever we work with others, we must maintain an engaging and welcoming interpersonal atmosphere (known as Psychological Safety) or others won't engage with us on a meaningful level. To do this, we need to remember to foster three things in all our communication modes (e.g., speech, text, non-verbal, etc.):

➢ The Humility to realize and remember that no one can have a monopoly on truth.
➢ The Confidence to say what is most crucial and listen with an open mind.
➢ The Skill to speak the unspeakable and leave each other grateful for the honesty.

It is important to realize that you will communicate with people who do not, or forget to, foster these three things. That does not excuse you from behaving in a way that maintains psychological safety, if you really want to recover the conversation and achieve anything meaningful.

Tip 36. Your communication competency during conflicts is very memorable

We exhibit more communication competency and have more impact when we follow a process that encompasses all the best practices summarized by Patterson (2002) as, "S.T.A.T.E. My Path."

➢ Share your facts first (facts are the least insulting).
➢ Tell your story (briefly focus on the most salient concern and avoid overkilling it). The goal of your story should be to expand your shared understanding, not to prove a point.
➢ Ask for others' paths (i.e., their facts and story).
➢ Talk with an open mind and do not disguise your beliefs or opinions as fact. Admit you might not have the whole picture but that you are interested in building a better one.
➢ Encourage the testing of your ideas and constructive criticism. The more others see that you want to play openly with the information in order to come to a better understanding, the more willing they will be to consider your needs, wants, and proposals.

Professionals who follow these best practices, even under duress and during complex challenges, are more likely to be remembered as competent, and subsequently promoted, than professionals who violate these practices.

The book referenced is:

Patterson, K. (2002). Crucial conversations: Tools for talking when stakes are high. Tata McGraw-Hill Education.

Tip 37. Use Strong Beliefs as a RED FLAG for Yourself

The more certain we feel, the more likely we are to move out of dialogue and into debate. When we feel the need to push our ideas on others, it's generally because we believe we're right and everyone else is wrong. Then we feel justified in using dirty tricks and indulging in the damaging cognitive biases and fallacies that derail entire careers. For example, the Straw Man fallacy of setting up an imaginary "worst case scenario" and then defending against that instead of dealing with reality as it currently exists.

To DO BETTER when you find yourself trying to convince others your way is best:

➢ Back off your current attack and think about what you really want for the relationship.
➢ Learn to look/ watch for the moment when people start to resist or show signs of fatigue or frustration with the conversation.
➢ Try to tone down your approach by bringing your non-verbal behaviors back to neutral and change your focus to your observations on your own functioning (instead of on the broader topic).

106

➤ If you're starting to feel indignant, or can't figure out why others can't see your point of view then ask for a timeout.

The book reference is:

Stone, D., Heen, S., & Patton, B. (2010). Difficult conversations: How to discuss what matter s most Penguins.

Tip 38. Dissolving Tension with "Difficult" People at Work

The tension in my spine builds in mere nanoseconds as I overhear Fred talk with a colleague down the hall. I didn't have the stomach to read the email he sent last night and I suck in a deep breath as I imagine what he will say when he makes it down the hall to my office. Fred and I seem to be at polar- opposites in our communication style, work habits, personality, and values. It's amazing how quickly the level of stress ratchets up when he's around!

I accept the fact that I'm going to get along with some people more easily than others at work and that I don't have to see "eye to eye" with everyone. In fact, more than a few important benefits to organizations are available only when there is diversity among its members. However, when a key stakeholder (e.g., boss, primary customer) differs dramatically from us, it's easy for misunderstandings and hard feelings to build, then cast a negative "cloud" over almost any interaction. In addition, the human tendency to seek out evidence that confirms an initial impression doesn't help (e.g., I believe that Fred is inconsiderate of my time, so I'm much more likely to remember times when he's late to meetings than when he volunteers to work over the weekend to help someone out of a bind). That is one reason why it's so easy for a negative and self-reinforcing cycle to develop and noticeably add to the stress already involved in work.

This negative cycle can demand significant time and energy and keep the frustration level high. When you find yourself in this position, here are four things you can do to turn this negative dynamic around:

1) **Focus on the positives.** Make a list of Fred's positive characteristics, both on the professional and personal sides. For example, Fred has an impressive store of organizational knowledge as a 20- year veteran, and he excels at solving customer problems. He participates on numerous cross- functional teams and also maintains a commitment to several charitable organizations. As a result, he is spread pretty thin, and sometimes things fall through the cracks. Come up with at least 5 positive characteristics for the "Fred" in your life and review it when the frustration starts to build. If you have trouble generating this list based upon your personal views of your "Fred," consider what other people appreciate about him.

2) **If you spot it, you got it!** Consider whether Fred annoys you so much because you share some of his weaknesses or bad habits. It's easy for me to conveniently forget times when I let a deadline slide because I had something I considered more important to do, or when I stepped out of meetings

that I didn't think pertained to me to make a phone call. How might others have interpreted my behavior then? Are Fred and I *really* all that different?

3) **Find and own your part.** Then it's time to challenge yourself to be brutally honest about what you are doing to contribute to the situation. Am I asking Fred for deliverables on short notice without considering how difficult it may be for him to reprioritize his other responsibilities? Am I changing the requirements for products or letting the scope of my request creep beyond what he originally agreed to? Am I asking for more from Fred without offering to give something in return? As much as I hate to admit it, I play a role in creating every situation that I don't like and I'm responsible for doing what I can to change it.

4) **Assume benign motives.** Finally, even if all of my complaints about Fred are "legitimate," Fred is not staying up until the wee hours of the morning plotting about ways to make my life miserable. Like me and most members of the human race, he is imperfect and is simply doing the best that he can. Using a compassionate lens to view the situation will help you get through the day with more of your sanity intact.

Tip 39 Know your unconscious bias

Our brains are exquisitely skilled in observing co-variation in the world. When we see time and time again that the presence of dark clouds precedes the fall of rain, we learn to associate clouds and rain. The repeated exposure to this covariation means that over time, an implicit cognitive association is formed between these two concepts…such that when I say dark clouds, others might even look up in anticipation of rain we would expect to follow.

This type of association often helps us navigate the world around us but can become problematic when we start to form these co-variations based on cultural expectations about others that are different from us. These co-variations are what form biases and just as dark clouds don't always indicate rain is coming, so too are many of our unconscious biases about others inaccurate.

It's important to remember that we all have biases (and these are formed by our culture, experience, personal connections, etc.) and these biases may affect our behavior. But by being aware of our biases and their influence, we can take steps to change those behaviors to reduce our bias through education and increasing exposure of other people, places, and things.

Check out our Prezi presentation to learn more about Unconscious Bias and what you can do to reduce your own bias:

http://prezi.com/smipvsl7jreq/?utm_campaign=share&utm_medium=copy

And if you want to assess your own unconscious bias, visit Harvard's Implicit Association Test:

www.implicit.harvard.edu.

TIP 40 REMEMBER THAT PERSONALITY CHANGES

We talk a lot about personality and the importance of personality influencing the success of an employee's performance on the job. Although considered stable, we know that personality does change over time. Check out this rather amazing article that suggests it may change more than we thought:

You're a completely different person at 14 and 77. The longest -running personality study ever has found, that over the course of a lifetime, "just as your physical appearance changes and your cells are constantly replaced, your personality is also transformed beyond recognition."

So, what does it all mean? For starters, this study strongly supports the notion of being open to change (for yourself and for others). Research like this may help us create more space for others and their changing views, behaviors, personalities. And this notion makes sense; our lives are enriched by experience. Why wouldn't this experience change our views, thoughts, and who we are?

Take today and consider how you can start to be more open to change and recognize that change within yourself.

The study referenced is:

113

Harris, M.A., Brett, C.E., Johnson, W., & Deary, I.J. (2016). Personality Stability From Age 14 to Age 77 Years,. Phsychology and Aging, 31 (8), 862

TIP 41 PSYCHO-SAFETY WORK SMARTS

Several factors contribute to mishaps, accidents, and unsafe working conditions. <u>Many of these contributing factors are psychological and social biases.</u> The good news is that you can do something about most of these biases—even when you're working in an organization with an unsafe culture.

The first way to counter biases and unsafe psychological influences is to learn about them. Just learning and being aware of their existence weakens their influence on your behaviors. Here are some of the most common biases and unsafe psychological influences to be aware of:

> ➢ **Diffusion of Responsibility**: your sense of responsibility diminishes in the presence of other people. People in a group are less likely to respond to an emergency than one person alone, because everyone in the group believes someone else will take care of it (or be better at taking care of it).
> ➢ **Pluralistic Ignorance**: when nobody else acts like anything is wrong, then you are more likely to believe or act like nothing is wrong (even when it is).

➢ **Deindividuation**: as part of a crowd you will feel more like you can hide impulsive or lazy behaviors that lead to unsafe working conditions.

➢ **Group-think**: in a group you will feel more pressured to go with the flow and agree with the rest of the group without talking things through.

➢ **Illusion of Transparency**: we grossly over-estimate others' ability to know what we are thinking and why.

➢ **Choice-supportive Bias**: once we make a choice, we convince ourselves that choice was made based on more evidence or information than it actually was.

➢ **Gambler's Fallacy**: we think that future probabilities are altered by past events, when in reality they are unchanged. For example, "I've safely skipped this step the last hundred times I did this, so there is no real chance skipping this step again will cause any trouble today."

What else can you do to keep yourself and your friends safe on the job?

1) **Slow things down.** Rarely do you really need to make a split second decision, but with other people around you're more likely to feel rushed into acting due to perceived social pressures (e.g. you don't want to keep a customer waiting, or look like an idiot who doesn't know how to start the procedure on your own). But you can combat errors before they

occur if you take an extra minute to think through things before acting. You can even invite those waiting on you to help you think it through and maximize your ability to avoid errors.

2) **Recruit certainty.** If you are unsure, consult the directions, manuals, a guru, an instructor, or a co-worker with knowledge, experience, and commitment to safe work practices. Asking for first-aid is far more embarrassing than asking for help or someone to look over your shoulder and help you make sure you're doing it right.

3) **Play devil's advocate.** We're programmed to go along with the crowd, but when we do so we miss plausible concerns that we could have done something about before they were catastrophic. Think about what might go wrong and make an explicit decision to deal with or ignore the risks.

4) **Take responsibility.** Don't assume someone else will notice or say something is amiss. If something feels or looks off, talk about it until others have at least acknowledged they see it too. If someone suggests doing something that is outside of or goes against your training, say you are not comfortable doing it and propose other options.

5) **Role-play responses.** Mentally rehearse or practice with a friend what you would do if someone pressured you to do unsafe work. We often commit to unsafe acts because we are put on the spot and don't have time to think of good responses or alternative options. Practicing what you would do

and say in such situations will make it a lot easier to make safe decisions. Practicing with others also models safe work for everyone.

TIP 42 GET BETTER AT LEAVING STRESSFUL WORKLOADS AT WORK

Research says when stressful workloads, and the unfinished tasks these workloads breed, persist in following you home (and even to bed) the quickest way to find relief is to use a daily planning diary before you punch out. Not all daily planning diaries are created equal though. There are **three keys** to making one work for you if you want to get that nagging task-anxiety monkey off your back:

1) Indicate in as much detail as possible **HOW** you think you will complete each unfinished task (e.g. using these materials provided by this expert, with help from this nurse manager or that construction supervisor, in this application with data from that spreadsheet, etc.).

2) Note each task's deadline; but even more importantly be honest about **WHEN** you think you can finish the task. If there is a negative discrepancy between the two this gives you a chance to plan how you will handle it (e.g. bargain for an extension, ask for help, re-prioritize tasks, etc.)

3) Indicate **WHERE** you plan to complete the task (e.g. at home, on that flight to Detroit, in the client's offices, on the shop floor, at tomorrow's patient handover tag-up, etc.). This assigns a physical anchor to the task in your mind that allows you to stop worrying about it until you get to that location.

From our coaching and team building experiences, we've also found that noting or discussing these three things at the end of your shift also enables you to proactively spot and obtain the resources you will need to accomplish your tasks well before you're so desperate that it makes you sick to your stomach.

TIP 43 NEGOTIATE A BETTER SALARY FROM THE START

Negotiating just $5,000 more on an initial salary offer of $50,000 results in over a million dollars in lifetime earnings when you get the standard 2-3% yearly raise. And yet, over 50% of professionals don't even try to negotiate beyond their initial salary offer. Most people cite purely emotional/ psychological reasons for not asking for more money like: "I'm afraid they'll rescind the offer or go with another applicant," or "I don't even know how to go about asking for more without sounding too pushy." If this sounds like you, then we have some coaching tips from psychological research on negotiating salaries to help you out (and into greater earnings):

1) Find out what others like you who do that work (not Just that job title) in your area in that industry working for similar sized organizations make each year. Does education or experience make much difference? Ask around, search the web, and visit https://www.onetonline.org/ to see what the US Department of Labor says salaries are for that job in your city and state.

2) Find your courage and be politely casual. This is a lot easier when you get some coaching and have a

chance to role play your approach. Research shows that the majority of recruiters and employers have no problem whatsoever with a potential hire asking if there is any room to negotiate. If they say no, then thank them for letting you know. If they say yes, then...

3) Use good negotiating tactics. If the employer wants to know your salary expectations, turn the question around on them by saying you're somewhat flexible depending on the total package and work environment, and then ask what salary range they hope to hire within. When you do name your terms, suggest a precise amount like $4,819 or $5,075 higher than the range they provided, rather than a round amount (like $5,000). Research shows this leads the recruiter to think that you're well informed about the market and/ or your salary needs and that you're not just trying to up the price arbitrarily however you can.

4) Consider the total package and work environment. Remember that this is your time to gather information on the organization too and find out if you really want to work for them. Is it more important to you to have three weeks of vacation than it is to earn $3,545 more per year or vice versa? Is it more important to you to have a new high-performance laptop and smartphone every two years than it is to have your own office? You may want to negotiate these things instead of or as a part of your salary negotiations.

Tip 44 Be a star interviewee

Most competency and behavior-based job interviews want you to show case how your past experiences and actions demonstrate your fit for the job in question. The best way to do this well is to give the interviewer the information they need to make a sound judgment about you; and the easiest way to that is to use the very same "situation, task, action, result" (STAR) format that good interview questions are based on. When an interviewer asks you to describe a time when, tell a story about, or given an example, then make sure your answer includes:

1) A description of the **situation** and why it was challenging or how it relates to the job you're interviewing for now.
2) A summary of the **tasks** you were assigned or required to achieve. Especially those tasks that contributed to the situation's ultimate progress or resolution.
3) A statement describing the **action** you took to handle those tasks, including why you decided on that action.

4) A report of the **results** of your actions that may include what outcome resulted for you, your co-workers, your customers, and your organization immediately and in the end. It never hurts to describe what you learned as a result, too.

One final point, a good interview is just a systematic and semi-structured conversation which aims to get to know the candidate (i.e. you) better; so good responses are those that help the interviewer get to know how well you fit the job. But don't forget, a good interview is a two-way conversation that should also help you learn what sore of actions and behaviors are important for the job so that you can gauge if the job really fits your interests and skills too.

TIP 45 JOB ANALYSIS?

Don't worry, it's not a dirty word, but it is something you should know about if you work with people or must build a team. Job analysis is a systematic study of the tasks, duties, and responsibilities of a job and the qualities (knowledge, skills, abilities, personal characteristics, competencies) needed to perform it. The results of a job analysis study are used to build evidence-based job descriptions.

Who must do a Job Analysis and Why?

Legally, every organization with 15 or more employees needs a job analysis in order to show their selection, promotion, compensation, training, and development practices are fair and job-related. Practically speaking, **all organizations** need a job analysis study to build the accurate job descriptions that enable efficient business operations and planning. For example, a good job description defines the tasks that are minimally required for anyone to be successful in that job with your organization.

Job analyses are also useful for: clarifying team roles, promoting safe work behaviors, maximizing disaster preparedness, finding opportunities to streamline and improve product and service delivery, forecasting recruitment needs, succession planning and organizational development, specifying certification and educational standards, identifying solutions to training gaps, differentiating your business in a competitive market, and facilitating change management. In addition to the legal, ethical, and practical/financial benefits of doing job analyses, we also frequently see businesses gain socio-emotional returns with their employees, customers, and communities (who are impressed that your business takes the time to understand and craft jobs within your organization).

How is Job Analysis done?

There are many acceptable study methods for conducting a job analysis, but the "multi-method" approach is the most ideal because it provides richer information to support an organization's business decisions. The multi-method approach uses more than one of the following methodologies to collect information about the job:

➢ Interviews with managers, supervisors, job incumbents, previous job-holders, and/ or customers
➢ Focus groups
➢ Surveys
➢ Observations or Ride-Alongs
➢ Analytical Reviews of public information about the job (e.g. trade magazines, the Department of

Labor's job descriptions and salary definitions for that job, job postings listed by competing organizations)

How long does it take and how much does it cost?

The time that it takes to complete a job analysis (which determines how much it costs) depends on the number of people in your business who are working that job. As a general rule of thumb, it takes an analyst two to seven days to complete job analysis for a job with up to 30 employees, one to three weeks for a job with 30 to 50 employees, and four to six weeks for a job with more than 50 employees. More than one job analysis may be conducted simultaneously (saving time and money), or a team of two or more analysts may also be used to reduce time and labor costs.

The real reasons for job analysis

To build a consistently successful employee recruiting process, selection/ promotion system, performance appraisal, training program, or compensation system, you must know exactly what is required to perform your jobs successfully.

In fact, job analysis forms the basis for solving just about every Human Resources problem and challenge. Detailed job descriptions and job specifications help you legally, efficiently, and ethically decide what is truly fair and equal pay, what is a reasonable accommodation, what is a minimum qualification, what is a strategic performance benchmark, and what succession and knowledge management plans are most critical to your organization. Job analysis also illuminates the motivators and demotivators inherent in your location, organization, and operating context allowing job incumbents to more fully master their own professional development and achieve their career dreams.

TIP 46 AVOID THE "JUSTS"

What actually motivates most of us to achieve? Psychology says it is the intrinsic rewards that actually keep us drudging through the details on the worst days and make our best days at work really sing. More specifically, the psychological rewards we value most are autonomy, flow, mastery, purpose, relationships, and acknowledgement. **Autonomy** in the work place means the ability to behave independently, to do things on one's own, in particular to decide how a task is done or a problem is approached given a set of performance expectations. **Flow** is the mental state you experience when you are so focused on the task at hand that the rest of the world fades away, it is total engagement in the moment. **Mastery** is comprehensive knowledge of a subject or skill and the recognition of our expertise or skill level. **Purpose** means a personal reason or belief in the importance of our work and purpose generally drives our pride in the work. Research shows that purpose is also what helps us decide if our career is a calling. Folks who work at their calling are significantly healthier, happier, and more resilient and live higher quality lives for longer on average than people who never get to work at a calling. In regard to **relationships**, we don't have to like the people we work for or with, but it does help us feel motivated to do difficult tasks. We don't want to let our friends down and we like having people needing/ wanting us to work with them. At the very least we need polite and productive relationships with the people we work for and with or we become demotivated faster than we do when we are missing any other of these intrinsic rewards. The most important part of a bonus or a raise, as it turns out, is when it serves as formal **acknowledgement** of our efforts and achievements. We want someone, preferably our boss or a leader we respect, to express sincere gratitude for our work. Written acknowledgement that we can refer back to when we need an emotional booster is especially effective—even if it is just a spoken thank you that we wrote down ourselves to remember.

In short, avoid falling for 3 Crummy "Justs":

1) Don't just write down your goals each year. Do analyze your strengths, opportunities, aspirations, and resources well enough to write down SMART goals and create an Action Priority Matrix. Do update it in writing at least once a quarter.
2) Don't just "do your best." Set specific and challenging goals (SMART goals). Identify metrics, red flags, and checkpoints for yourself so you can monitor your progress and know when to ask for help.

3) Don't just visualize success. Visualize all the steps you will take to make success happen. Imagine your efforts failed and identify the most likely reason your efforts failed so that you can plan how to spot it and avoid or mitigate it ahead of time.

TIP 47 GRATITUDE GAINS

We often hear that keeping a gratitude journal or trying out other ways to add more gratitude into your life has many positive personal benefits (physically, mentally, and emotionally). Research backs that up. In it, she outlines some very specific benefits of cultivating a culture of gratitude in the workplace, such as: increases job satisfaction, decreases burnout, more openness to new ideas, and more prosocial behavior (e.g., picking up that trash someone else left in the kitchen or bringing donuts into work one morning for the team).

In fact, employees who engaged in gratitude practice at work increased their positivity (their tendency to look at incidents or issues as either positive or negative) and they had a greater sense of workplace community. Not surprisingly, cultivating gratitude has some serious outcomes both personally and professionally. To create a culture of gratitude, you can make a habit of listing and having your teams list and describe things you are grateful for at team meetings, retreats, or as a quick opener in more frequent staff meetings.

And if you want to know more about positive psychology research on gratitude, check out these references:

Watkins, P. C., Woodward, K., Stone, T. & Kolts, R. L. (2003). Gratitude and happiness: Development of a measure of gratitude, and relationships with subjective well-being. Behaviour and Personality, 31 (5), 431-452.

Dunn, J. R. & Schweitzer, M. E.(2005). Feeling and Believing: The Influence of Emotion on Trust. Journal of Personality and Social Psychology, 88(5), 736-748. doi:10.1037/0022-3514.88.5.736

Wood, A. M., Maltby, J., Gillett, R., Linley, P. A., & Joseph, S. (2008). The role of gratitude in the development of social support, stress, and depression: Two longitudinal studies. Journal of Research in Personality, 42, 854–871.

TIP 48 AMPLIFICATION, OR HOW TO GET HEARD

Frustrated that your voice is not heard, you are not recognized or given credit for your work, or your ideas are being taken by someone else? Do something about it: consider the concept of amplification, a strategy in which individuals work together to ensure recognition is given appropriately and accurately.

What is amplification

Let's consider an example. According to a Washington Post article, Obama female staffers were frustrated with their lack of recognition for their contribution and inclusion in important meetings and decisions at the beginning of his first term. To address this, these staffers utilized amplification and "made sure in every meeting that once a woman in the room made a key point other women would repeat it, giving credit to its author. This forced the men in the room to recognize the contribution — and denied them the chance to claim the idea as their own." And it worked. At the start of Obama's first term in 2009, about two-third of his top staffers were men. By his second term, staff gender was represented equally among men and women.

134

This is not just a tactic to be used my women in the work place. This can be used by anybody that feels frustrated with the way in which their contributions are being recognized at work. So... how to put this in action? Start by connecting with others that you work with; share this idea and agree to jointly acknowledge each other using amplification in meetings to encourage equality and individual contribution. And then do it and see what happens. You and your colleagues will not only see a difference fair recognition. This level of support for each other will also improve teamwork support and your team's cohesion (which has some pretty great effects on performance as well).

Tip 49 Enhance your Intrinsic Motivation

Lots of us work hard to master difficult jobs and achieve status at work only to find that, well, it just isn't as satisfying as we thought it was going to be. We need something more to find or encourage our motivation again, specifically we want something to enhance our intrinsic motivation (you know, that personal passion you sometimes feel for conquering challenges). Psychological research has a few tips for helping us get our groove back instead of lolling in these lulls, and we'd like to share them with you.

For starters, work on creating "Transformative" Experiences" Experiences that allow you to see new perspectives and try out serving different purposes deepens your knowledge of yourself and hence improves your personal and professional autonomy. For example, volunteering to be "finance person" for one project instead of taking on your normal project role. Or shadowing a colleague, who does a job you're totally unfamiliar or uneducated to do, for a few hours.

Also, master your learning orientation so you experience more flow. Praise yourself for going out on a limb to learn new things. What makes failing and trying again just as interesting as actually achieving something for you? What kind of learning do you get so involved in that you forget to go home at quitting time? This experience of "flow" and being excited about learning something is another primary intrinsic motivator and there is probably some aspect of your current job that you already experience flow around and could build on.

In the beginning, do what you enjoy most first and you'll keep going. For folks who enjoying losing weight by dieting more than they do by exercising, losing the first ten pounds by dieting results in mastering both dieting and exercising sooner and losing and keeping off more weight. This is one way of acknowledging and using your own history of success to fuel you farther. A sense of accomplishment is motivating, even if the accomplishments are small. For example, if you're trying to manage time better on the job and you like using technology more than you like cleaning your desk, start by keeping your electronic calendar application up to date for a week first before adding the initiative to clear your desk before leaving work every day.

Spend more time figuring out what went well (that you should repeat or leverage, or savor) than you do figuring out what you didn't do well or didn't like (and need to fix). Leveraging strengths is like using super powers and leads to mastery much sooner than correcting weaknesses (sometimes impossible anyway). This is another practical way of acknowledging your own efforts and gaining a feeling of accomplishment. Take two minutes at the end of each work day to write down one thing you did or tried that work well that day and soon you will have a library of tactics that work at work.

Finally, enlist lots of social support and peer pressure. If your teammate expects to see you at that public speaking class, then you are 50 times more likely to show up to the class even if you're exhausted. When others know your goals and see your progress first hand, they are also a lot more likely to sincerely acknowledge and praise your efforts, thus increasing your feelings of recognition and accomplishment. Whatever your work goals, be sure to share each goal with at least one colleague or mentor so they can be your cheerleader, or a task-master as needed.

TIP 50 GIVE YOURSELF THE LUXURY OF TRANSFORMATIVE EXPERIENCES

Transformative experiences ignite our passions and ensure our work-life satisfaction. Here are ten ways you can find and create more transformative experiences for yourself.

1) **Add New Dimensions to Your Current Position**
Think outside your formal job description when seeking out new challenges. The first place to start may be helping your coworkers jettison unpleasant tasks from their plates. Consider moving a responsibility from someone else's plate to your own, trading tasks with another, or taking on a role or task that no one currently owns. Expand your repertoire of skills and responsibilities while also helping your colleagues. Join safety, quality, environmental, ethics, budget, etc. committees within the organization to gain more exposure to different aspects or divisions of work. Talk to one other professional each week to learn how others around you think about managing work, developing business, developing people, building careers (e.g.

what is work in/ on X all about, what works well in your experience, what was easy/ hard to learn for you, how do you teach others X, how do you monitor production/ profits/ quality/ safety, etc.) and take the time to think about how to leverage this information to make your own job ever more meaningful

2) **Use Short-Term Assignments to Fuel Long-Term Growth**
The best way to ensure that you follow through on practicing new tasks and responsibilities and vary your experiences is with short-term or temporary projects. One-offs allow you to learn while also giving you the freedom to pursue other opportunities as soon as each assignment is completed. You'll learn whether you enjoy the work as well as improve your professional record for seeing things to fruition.

3) **Start Informal Apprenticeships and Shadowing**
Interview and observe colleagues already working in the job and at the levels that interest you (e.g. what did they need to know the first day on the job, what career path brought them there, how do they develop people and business in this role, how do they redesign/ customize the job to fit, etc.). Arrange a project or period to work with and learn from colleagues who have mastered a knowledge area or skill you need to get to your next level.

4) **Use Mindfulness to Find Meaning**
If you're not savoring this part of the learning journey, then getting past it is going to suck. Mindfulness is

140

simply focusing on how things feel, smell, taste, sound, or impact you right now. When we do so, we're happier—even when we're doing so in an isolated and confined work environment.

5) **Pursue opportunities outside of the office.** Nonprofit, religious, social, and professional organizations, school, sports teams, and family life also offer us alternative outlets for transformative and interesting experience when we're limited at work. Special interest groups (e.g., Toastmasters), innovation centers, incubator groups, and even online internship listings also offer us chances to get some transformative work related experience on our own when our organizations can't afford to provide them;

6) **Get a village of informal mentors.** A library of mentors (i.e, friends willing to watch you in your work situations) can give you behavior-based feedback in specific areas of expertise, and inspire you with war stories to make work more interesting and keep our personal development progressing even while our job title is fixed.

Bonus Tip Find the right coach for you

As a society, we take our physical health seriously. At a minimum, most people would consider getting an annual physical a necessity and now more than ever, most folks participate in some kind of physical exercise to maintain an improved level of physical fitness (according to a 2013 US News World & Report article, Americans spend north of $60 billion annually trying to lose weight). Closely related, individuals are spending more than ever before to improve aspects of their own psychological well-being (according to a report from ABC news, Americans spend about $55 billion every year on psychotherapy and medication).

Considering you spend a large chunk of your life at work every day (with an average workday of eight hours, most Americans are spending at least 30% of their lives in a work environment), then why would you not consider taking advantage of coaching to improve multiple aspects of your work life and satisfaction?

Ample research evidence shows that employees who engage in coaching see improvements in job satisfaction, improved performance on the job, and an increased effectiveness in achieving career goals.

142

Like the idea of consulting with a medical doctor about your physical health or a personal fitness trainer about your physical fitness and exercise regimen, a coach provides you with critical insights about yourself as a professional (what we call your Knowledge, Skills, Abilities, and Orientations or KSAOs). A coach helps you identify the job and career you want, and gain the tools you need to reach your work goals. A lot of coaching is about finding out what time it is in your career and where your professional development is in relation to that schedule (so to speak), then developing a plan to get you where you want to be on time.

Look specifically for coaching services customized to fit your needs— whether that's aligning your abilities and personal interests with your career path (FOCUS), understanding your strengths to maintain your current professional path (MAINTAIN), identifying key areas you can professionally develop to improve your career (IMPROVE), or rapidly accelerating your professional growth (ACCELERATE).

ABOUT THE AUTHORS/ COACHES

Kathryn E. Keeton, Ph.D.

Kathryn is an expert in innovation and strategic management within organizations. She has experience coaching professionals and developing teams and leaders in some of the most extreme working environments on (as well as off) earth.

William S. O'Keefe, M.S.

Bill served over twenty years as a USAF pilot and instructor before spending another twenty years managing, designing, and delivering team training to astronauts and flight controllers at NASA.

Lacey L. Schmidt, Ph.D.

Lacey has provided selection, training, and development systems to organizations for a variety of interesting jobs and work teams, including: astronauts, firefighters, police detectives, nurses, chefs, financial advisers, engineers, pilots, and Antarctic expeditioners.

Kelley J. Slack, Ph.D.

Kelley has spent over twenty years providing insight into organizations' customers, employees, and culture through surveys. Her work recognizes the interrelationship between what work means to employees and how organizations make decisions.

Annette Spychalski, Ph.D.

Annette holds an Associate Certified Coach credential from the International Coaching Federation, and has over two decades of experience in coaching, assessment, team facilitation, training, multi- rater feedback, and development.

LEARN MORE

If you're an individual looking for a career adviser or more advice on developing professionally:

www.coachingpeoplewise.com
#careerwiser

If you're a leader looking for more advice on building engaged and talented teams:

www.thewisdomthatworks.com
inquiry@thewisdomthatworks.com

1-888-661-7874
#workwiser

www.ingramcontent.com/pod-product-compliance
Lightning Source LLC
Chambersburg PA
CBHW060034210326
41520CB00009B/1125